ACTS OF THE APOSTLES:

DISPENSATIONALLY CONSIDERED

A GRACE EXPOSITIONAL COMMENTARY

SECOND EDITION

DR. DAVID ALAN GREENE

GraceWord Publishing, LLC
www.gracewordpublishing.com
U.S.A.

Contents

To Dr. Nathan Killian and his wife Jeanette

Be it known therefore unto you,
that the salvation of God
is sent unto the Gentiles,
and that they will hear it.

Acts 28:28

Acknowledgements

To all who love God's Son, the Word of God, more than they love their customs and traditions. For they have put aside their religious beliefs and make the Word of God their sole authority. You spur me on and give me a reason to write.

I would like to thank Jon and Susan McMahon for their encouragement. For their work in the editing process, I would like to thank Barbara Pennington, Frances Greene, and Greg Isaacs.

1

An Historical Perspective

Much can be said about this book entitled The Acts of the Apostles. First, it establishes a timeline beginning with Christ's resurrection. Second, it is a book which is transitional because it takes us from one place and brings us to another. It begins in the Age of Law. It ends in the Age of Grace. Luke records this in a way that a medical doctor would pay attention to the details. He takes us with him through the historical events following Christ's death, burial, and resurrection. Luke recorded these events as an eyewitness. He was there.

Acts begins as the continuation of the four gospels. It places us in Jerusalem amidst the turmoil of the persecution that followed. In mid-Acts, we are introduced to someone who was never before mentioned in the Bible. Saul pursues the new Kingdom Believers. He was an enemy of these new believers, but also an enemy of Jesus Christ as he persecuted His followers. Luke records the events surrounding his involvement in the oppression that caused many Kingdom Believers to scatter and go into hiding.

The Acts of the Apostles takes us from the Gospel of the Kingdom preached by Christ and His Twelve to a turning point. It should be seen as a watershed moment in the New Testament. As in a great play, the lights dim at the end of the first act. In the next act, as the lights grow brighter, the scene is different. We are introduced to a new main character Saul. This man pursued the followers of Christ and is later confronted by Him. Saul's powerful conversion is found in Acts. Later, we are told learn that God set him aside for His Own purpose.

I say that the Acts of the Apostles is a transitional book for a reason. We will look at the details shortly. For now, let me summarize this point. Jesus Christ's earthly ministry involved the Twelve Apostles. He lived with them and taught them as they accompanied Him throughout His three-year ministry. Stephen was one of these followers and the first martyr. He gives an historic speech before the Jewish rulers and details for them their long history of fighting against God. They commit the one sin that

Christ said would not be forgiven. They rush upon Stephen and stone him. Here, we are introduced to Saul who would later become the Apostle Paul.

Luke now begins to follow Paul's life and ministry. In fact, Luke actually accompanied Paul on much of his missionary journeys. I would like to offer a suggestion. (As we follow Paul on his missionary trips, there is an excellent online source of Bible maps" www.bibleatlas.org. All you need to do is enter the name of the city or place.) This allows us to experience first-hand the moving of God his life. Paul begins his ministry by going "to the Jews first and also to the Gentiles" (Rom. 1:16, 2:9-10). Early in his ministry he preached to both the Jew and the Gentile. However, their constant rejection, which was sometimes violent, would cause him, in the end, to go almost exclusively to the Gentiles.

At the close of Acts, Paul makes this proclamation: "Be it known therefore unto you, that the salvation of God is sent unto the Gentiles, and that they will hear it" (Acts 28:28). Therefore, by the end of Acts, this historic transition is now complete. The thirteen books that follow the book of Acts are Paul's epistles. These were written by the man whom God had appointed to be the Apostle to the Gentiles.

2

Acts 1

We do not have much information on the author of the book of Acts. We do know that Luke wrote both the Gospel of Luke as well as the Acts of the Apostles. He was a physician. It is believed that he was Greek. However, Paul credits the Jews for being the guardians of Scripture. So, I believe, Luke was a Grecian Jew. His profession gave him exceptional knowledge of the Greek language. This allowed him to record these events in the common language at the time.

Luke begins by continuing the narrative recorded in the four gospels. He mentions his treatise, the Gospel of Luke, which he had completed. The name, Theophilus, means "one who loved God" and is a reference to all who love the Lord Jesus Christ. Acts 1:1-2:

1 The former treatise have I made, O Theophilus, of all that Jesus began both to do and teach,

2 Until the day in which he was taken up, after that <u>he through the Holy Ghost had given commandments unto the apostles whom he had chosen</u>:

Jesus' earthly ministry ended with His Ascencion. Just prior to Him being taken up into the clouds, Jesus gave His Apostles, those present with Him, specific instructions.

Acts is a continuation of the four gospels. Nothing has changed dispensationally. His Apostles, present at His Ascension, receive instructions from Him. They are to teach the followers of the Kingdom Gospel to "do" something. Matthew 28:18-20:

18 And Jesus came and spake unto them, saying, All power is given unto me in heaven and in earth.

19 Go ye therefore, and teach all nations, <u>baptizing them</u> in the name of the Father, and of the Son, and of the Holy Ghost: 20 <u>Teaching them</u> to ob-

serve [do] all things whatsoever I have commanded you: and, lo, I am with you alway, even unto the end of the world. Amen.

Going forward, we will see that action or "doing" is a defining characteristic of the Gospel of the Kingdom. However, this would be contrary to the Gospel of Grace preached by Paul. Again, believers who follow the Gospel of the Kingdom must "observe" or "do" all that Jesus commanded His Twelve to do.

Luke continues by providing confirmation of the resurrection. Salvation for both gospels is based upon the resurrection of Jesus Christ. Most of those to whom Luke is writing were alive at that time. Many of them were eyewitnesses. Verse 3:

> 3 **To whom also he shewed himself alive after his passion by many infallible proofs, being seen of them forty days, and speaking of the things pertaining to the kingdom of God:**

These infallible or unquestionable proofs were Jesus' appearance among the people for the forty days leading up to His Ascension. While in their presence, He commanded His Apostles to remain in Jerusalem. Verse 4:

> **4 And [He], being assembled together with them, commanded them that they should not depart from Jerusalem, but wait for the promise of the Father, which, saith he, ye have heard of [from] me.**

Before His crucifixion, Jesus told them what would happen to Him. However, to comfort them in His impending absence, He assured them He would send them the Comforter. John 16:5-7:

> **5 But now I go my way to him that sent me; and none of you asketh me, Whither goest thou? 6 But because I have said these things unto you, sorrow hath filled your heart.**

> **7 Nevertheless I tell you the truth; It is expedient for you that I go away: for if I go not away, the Comforter will not come unto you; but if I depart, I will send him unto you.**

This Comforter is the Holy Spirit – also called the Holy Ghost. After forty days, the Spirit or Comforter would come. Act 1:5:

> 5 For John truly baptized with water;
> but ye shall be baptized with the Holy
> Ghost not many days hence.

Jesus fellowshipped with His Apostles for the forty days following His Resurrection. As they spent this time together, they talked with their Friend. Verses 6-7:

> 6 When they therefore were come to-
> gether, they asked of him, saying, Lord,
> wilt thou at this time restore again the
> kingdom to Israel? 7 And he said unto
> them, It is not for you to know the
> times or the seasons, which the Father
> hath put in his own power.

They asked a similar question previously. The establishment of the eternal kingdom promised to King David is connected to both His Return and the end of the world. (See Daniel 9.) Matthew 24:3:

> 3 And as he sat upon the mount of Ol-
> ives, the disciples came unto him pri-
> vately, saying, Tell us, when shall
> these things be? and what shall be the
> sign of thy coming, and of the end of

the world?

When Jesus responds to their question, he includes an interesting word. He used this word in the same manner before. Since it is significant to the interpretation of this verse, we must pause for an explanation. You see, the word "and" can be used as a time separator. Luke recorded Jesus' visit to the synagogue. It was at the very beginning of His earthly ministry and immediately followed His forty-day testing in the wilderness. Luke 4:16-20:

> 16 And he came to Nazareth, where he had been brought up: and, as his custom was, he went into the synagogue on the sabbath day, and stood up for to read.
>
> 17 And there was delivered unto him the book of the prophet Esaias. And when he had opened the book, he found the place where it was written,
>
> 18 The Spirit of the Lord is upon me, because he hath anointed me to preach the gospel to the poor; he hath sent me to heal the brokenhearted, to preach

deliverance to the captives, and recovering of sight to the blind, to set at liberty them that are bruised, 19 To preach the acceptable year of the Lord.

20 And he closed the book, and he gave it again to the minister, and sat down. And the eyes of all them that were in the synagogue were fastened on him.

What happened? Why was everyone looking at Him? It was because He stopped in the middle of the Scripture! As He sat down, He spoke. Verse 21:

21 And he began to say unto them, This day is this scripture fulfilled in your ears.

Look at the verses He read in Isaiah 61:1-2:

1 The Spirit of the Lord GOD is upon me; because the LORD hath anointed me to preach good tidings unto the meek; he hath sent me to bind up the brokenhearted, to proclaim liberty to the captives, and the opening of the prison to them that are bound;

2 To proclaim the acceptable year of the LORD, . . .

Jesus stopped mid-sentence and did not complete the remainder of the verse because it did not yet apply. Verse 2:

> **. . . and the day of vengeance of our God; to comfort all that mourn;**

Why did He do this? The latter portion of the prophecy would not happen until the Tribulation! There is a division of time here and it was separated by the word "and." Consider a woman who was born in London *and* raised her children in Boston. The word "and" does not imply that these two actions happened simultaneously. Consider the first two verses of Genesis. There is a huge gap of time between these two verses that encompassed a great span of time. The same applies here. He brought good tidings for Israel now during His earthly ministry. And . . . the judgment will come later.

Let us return to Jesus and the fellowship He was enjoying with His Kingdom Apostles. Speaking of the coming of the Comforter, He continues. Acts 1:8:

8 But ye shall receive power, after that the Holy Ghost is come upon you: <u>and</u> ye shall be witnesses unto me both in Jerusalem, and in all Judaea, and in Samaria, and unto the uttermost part of the earth.

Similar to the example just given, there is a time break after the word "and" used above. During Paul's visits to Jerusalem, he found the other Apostles still in Jerusalem. (See Galatians 1 and 2.) It will not be until the 144,000 witnesses are sent to proclaim the Gospel of the Kingdom that the latter portion of this prophecy will be fulfilled. This will be during the seven remaining years following the Rapture. During the Tribulation, these witness will proclaim the Kingdom Gospel: "Repent and be baptized for the Kingdom of God is at hand!" (See Revelation 7:4.)

Grace Believers, however, have the "ministry of reconciliation." Paul makes this distinction to those who are saved by grace through faith. 2 Corinthians 5:17-19:

17 Therefore if any man be in Christ, he is a new creature: old things are passed away; behold, all things are become new. **18** And all things are of God, who hath reconciled us to himself by Jesus Christ, **and hath given to us the ministry of reconciliation;** 19 To wit, that God was in Christ, reconciling the world unto himself, not imputing their trespasses unto them; **and hath committed unto us the word of reconciliation.**

If you find this surprising, do not be alarmed. We will see this distinction more clearly as we press on. Before His Ascension, Jesus was speaking to those He had entrusted with the Gospel of the Kingdom. They were taught during their time with Christ and were to carry the Gospel of the Kingdom to "the lost sheep of the house of Israel." Matthew 10:5-7:

> 5 These twelve Jesus sent forth, and commanded them, saying, **Go not into the way of the Gentiles,** and into any city of the Samaritans enter ye not: 6 **But go rather to the lost sheep of the house of Israel.** 7 And as ye go, preach, saying, **The kingdom of heaven is at hand.**

These Apostles had been with their Lord for three years. Now, they watched Him depart from them. Their hearts must have been filled with both awe and sadness. Their dear Friend was leaving them behind. However, He had assured them He would be with them always. He would send them the Comforter to console them, teach them, and remind them. Acts 1:9-11:

> 9 **And when he had spoken these things, while they beheld, he was taken up; and a cloud received him out of their sight.**

> 10 **And while they looked stedfastly toward heaven as he went up, behold, two men stood by them in white apparel;**

> 11 **Which also said, Ye men of Galilee, why stand ye gazing up into heaven? <u>this same Jesus, which is taken up from you into heaven, shall so come in like manner as ye have seen him go into heaven.</u>**

We can picture them standing there looking skyward. As He had left the earth, so would He also return. Here, the angel is speaking about the Second Coming. Jesus, as Israel's King, will return to rescue them. He will defeat their enemies who seek to destroy them. All this will happen at the end of the seven-year Tribulation.

Life continued for them as usual. As instructed, they waited for the promised Comforter. Verses 12-14:

> 12 Then returned they unto Jerusalem from the mount called Olivet, which is from Jerusalem a sabbath day's journey.

> 13 And when they were come in, they went up into an upper room, where abode both Peter, and James, and John, and Andrew, Philip, and Thomas, Bartholomew, and Matthew, James the son of Alphaeus, and Simon Zelotes, and Judas the brother of James.

> 14 These all continued with one accord in prayer and supplication, with the women, and Mary the mother of Jesus, and with his brethren.

There was the matter concerning the replacement of Judas. There must be twelve apostles Verses 15-20:

> 15 And in those days Peter stood up in the midst of the disciples, and said, (the number of names together were about an hundred and twenty,)

16 Men and brethren, this scripture must needs have been fulfilled, which the Holy Ghost by the mouth of David spake before concerning Judas, which was guide to them that took Jesus. 17 For he was numbered with us, and had obtained part of this ministry.

18 Now this man purchased a field with the reward of iniquity; and falling headlong, he burst asunder in the midst, and all his bowels gushed out. 19 And it was known unto all the dwellers at Jerusalem; insomuch as that field is called in their proper tongue, Aceldama, that is to say, The field of blood.

20 For it is written in the book of Psalms, Let his habitation be desolate, and let no man dwell therein: and his bishoprick let another take.

To find Judas' replacement, there were certain qualifications. Verses 21-22:

21 Wherefore of these men which have companied with us all the time that the Lord Jesus went in and out among us, 22 Beginning from the baptism of John,

unto that same day that he was taken up from us, must one be ordained to be a witness with us of his resurrection.

The Apostle Paul was unable to meet these qualifications. It was not an error or poor decision on the part of the other apostles. Later, we learn Paul does not met the other apostles until much later. It was not until after His Ascension that Paul met the Risen Savior. (See Galatians 1:15-19.) Two candidates were found that met the required qualifications. Verses 23-26:

> 23 **And they appointed two, Joseph called Barsabas, who was surnamed Justus, and Matthias. 24 And they prayed, and said, Thou, Lord, which knowest the hearts of all men, shew whether of these two thou hast chosen,**

> 25 **That he may take part of this ministry and apostleship, from which Judas by transgression fell, that he might go to his own place. 26 And they gave forth their lots; and the lot fell upon Matthias; and he was numbered with the eleven apostles.**

The number of apostles had been resolved. These twelve apostles along with the twelve sons of Jacob, called Israel, will reign in Christ's earthly Kingdom. We will see Christ, the descendant of King David and his legitimate Heir, will rule upon his throne in Jerusalem forever.

3

Acts 2

Pentecost is a Jewish holiday that comes fifty days after Passover. It is also known by another name: Festival of the First Fruits. It celebrates the beginning of the harvest. Do you recall in the Gospels that Jesus spoke about the harvest? This was in relation to saving the lost sheep of Israel. Matthew 9:36-38:

> 36 **But when he saw the multitudes, he was moved with compassion on them, because they fainted, and were scattered abroad, as sheep having no shepherd. 37 Then saith he unto his disciples, The harvest truly is plenteous, but the labourers are few;**
>
> 38 **Pray ye therefore the Lord of the harvest, that he will send forth labour-**

ers into his harvest.

Jesus mentions this "harvest" many times in the gospels. Due to the importance of understanding this harvest, let us consider Jesus' explanation to His twelve disciples. Matthew 13:36-40:

> 36 **Then Jesus sent the multitude away, and went into the house: and his disciples came unto him, saying, Declare [Explain] unto us the parable of the tares of the field. 37 He answered and said unto them, He that soweth the good seed is the Son of man;**
>
> 38 **The field is the world; the good seed are <u>the children of the kingdom</u>; but the tares are the children of the wicked one; 39 The enemy that sowed them is the devil; <u>the harvest is the end of the world</u>; and the reapers are the angels. 40 As therefore the tares are gathered and burned in the fire; so shall it be in the end of this world.**

The "children of the kingdom" are the children of Abraham. The harvest is a time of testing, trying, or proving of "true" Israel. This will be the Tribulation—Jacob's Time of Testing. All of this has to do with the end of the world as we know it. At that time, the arrival of the kingdom will be imminent! Jesus told them that "the kingdom was at hand." However, we will see a temporary suspension will occur. This causes a delay of the kingdom.

Most Christians are taught the "Church" began at Pentecost. This is not true. We must always examine the evidence! When we do, we will find no reference to Gentile believers here. These early events in Acts concerns only "the children of Abraham." This is still the Age of Law. Paul, the Apostle of the Gentiles, has not yet appeared.

The Lord directed the Apostles and the Kingdom Believers to wait for the Comforter. Acts 2:1-4:

> 1 **And when the day of Pentecost was fully come, they were all with one accord in one place.** 2 **And suddenly there came a sound from heaven as of a rushing mighty wind, and it filled all the house where they were sitting.**
>
> 3 **And there appeared unto them cloven tongues like as of fire, and it sat upon each of them.** 4 **And they were all filled with the Holy Ghost, and began to**

speak with other tongues, as the Spirit gave them utterance.

The physical manifestations were evidence or signs of this miraculous event. Jews expected miracles, signs, and wonders as proof of God's working. You could say they were God's authentication. Later, we will see that those saved by grace must rely solely upon His Word and believe.

This religious festival required that all Jewish adult males attend. Verses 5-8:

> 5 And there were dwelling at Jerusalem Jews, devout men, out of every nation under heaven.
>
> 6 Now when this was noised abroad, the multitude came together, and were confounded, because that every man heard them speak in his own language.
>
> 7 And they were all amazed and marvelled, saying one to another, Behold, are not all these which speak Galilaeans? 8 And how hear we every man in our own tongue, wherein we were born?

Devout Jews had come from all over the Roman Empire. They were Jews from countries far from Israel. It was a chance for the scattered Jews to reconnect with their brethren in the Promised Land. Luke lists some of the countries represented here. Verses 9-11:

9 Parthians, and Medes, and Elamites, and the dwellers in Mesopotamia, and in Judaea, and Cappadocia, in Pontus, and Asia, 10 Phrygia, and Pamphylia, in Egypt, and in the parts of Libya about Cyrene, and strangers of Rome, Jews and proselytes, 11 Cretes and Arabians, we do hear them speak in our tongues the wonderful works of God.

Notice that these Jews recognized the words spoken in their native language. This was God's intent. As we will see in a moment, this would fulfill a prophecy given to the children of Israel by the Prophet Joel!

As humans, we try to rationalize things we cannot explain. Here, they reason these men are drunk even though it was only nine o'clock in the morning. Verses 12-13:

12 And they were all amazed, and were in doubt, saying one to another, What meaneth this? **13** Others mocking said, These men are full of new wine.

Peter stands to address the crowd who had gathered to view this spectacle. Verses 14-16:

14 But Peter, standing up with the eleven, lifted up his voice, and said unto them, Ye men of Judaea, and all ye that dwell at Jerusalem, be this known unto you, and hearken to my words:

15 For these are not drunken, as ye suppose, seeing it is but the third hour of the day. **16** But [rather] this is that which was spoken by the prophet Joel;

As he begins to speak to the Jews gathered for the festival, notice that he recounts for them the prophecy given to Israel along with Israel's history of rejecting God. Friend, this context cannot be applied to anyone other than the children of Israel.

Picture this group of Jews growing in number as they stopped to listen to Peter speak. Out of curiosity, they were hushing others so they might hear the explanation of what was happening. Peter continues with Joel's prophecy. Verses 17-21:

> 17 And it shall come to pass in the last days, saith God, I will pour out of my Spirit upon all flesh: and your sons and your daughters shall prophesy, and your young men shall see visions, and your old men shall dream dreams:

> 18 And on my servants and on my handmaidens I will pour out in those days of my Spirit; and they shall prophesy:

> 19 And I will shew wonders in heaven above, and signs in the earth beneath; blood, and fire, and vapour of smoke: 20 The sun shall be turned into darkness, and the moon into blood, before that great and notable day of the Lord come:

> 21 And it shall come to pass, that whosoever shall call on the name of the Lord shall be saved.

At the beginning of Peter's speech, he said, "And it shall come to pass in the last days." The harvest

which was to come in the last days was now imminent. It could happen at any time! This is the Festival of the First Fruits. It celebrates the beginning of
"the harvest!"

Israel's history is recorded for us in the Old
Testament. It is filled with stories of their rebellion
and rejection of both God and His prophets. Israel
continuously demonstrates their lack of faith. This
is the reason for how God would choose to deal
with them in the future. Peter brings what I call an
"indictment" against them. He charges them with
lack of faith. Verses 22-23:

> 22 **Ye men of Israel**, hear these words;
> Jesus of Nazareth, **a man approved of**
> **God among you by miracles and won-**
> **ders and signs**, which God did by him
> in the midst of you, as ye yourselves
> also know:

> 23 Him, being delivered by the deter-
> minate counsel and foreknowledge of
> God, ye have taken, and by wicked
> hands have crucified and slain:

He refers to those in attendance as brethren. They
had received their promised Messiah, sent by God,
and they killed Him! However, in spite of that, God

raised Him from the dead because He was righteous according to the Law. Verses 24-26:

> **24 Whom God hath raised up, having loosed the pains of death: because it was not possible that he should be holden of it.**
>
> **25 For David speaketh concerning him, I foresaw the Lord always before my face, for he is on my right hand, that I should not be moved: 26 Therefore did my heart rejoice, and my tongue was glad; moreover also my flesh shall rest in hope:**

Hope comes from trusting in the promises of God.

King David was confident of the resurrection, not only for himself, but also for the Holy One Who is Christ the Messiah. Verses 27-29:

> **27 Because thou wilt not leave my soul in hell, neither wilt thou suffer thine Holy One to see corruption. 28 Thou hast made known to me the ways of life; thou shalt make me full of joy with thy countenance.**

29 Men and brethren, let me freely speak unto you of the patriarch David, that he is both dead and buried, and his sepulchre is with us unto this day.

Writing under the influence of the Holy Spirit, David remembers God's promise concerning the future of David's kingdom. It would be through David's greater Son that this promise would be fulfilled. God would raise up Christ to sit upon David's throne forever. Verses 30-32:

30 Therefore being a prophet, and knowing that God had sworn with an oath to him [David], that of the fruit of his loins, according to the flesh, he [God] would raise up Christ to sit on his [David's] throne;

31 He seeing this before spake of the resurrection of Christ, that his soul was not left in hell, neither his flesh did see corruption. **32** This Jesus hath God raised up, whereof we all are witnesses.

Remember, both His crucifixion, burial and resurrection occurred only fifty days prior to this festival. Many in the crowd were eyewitnesses to these events.

Peter tells them that the Christ, now exalted, sits at the right hand of God the Father Almighty. As promised, He sent the Comforter Who is the Holy Spirit. This is Peter's explanation of what they were now seeing and hearing. Verse 33:

> 33 **Therefore being by the right hand of God exalted, and [we] having received of [from] the Father the promise of the Holy Ghost, he hath shed forth this, which ye now see and hear.**

The Jews knew that David was not speaking about himself because his sepulcher was not far from where they were now standing. Peter refers to a psalm in which Elohim (the LORD) speaks to Adonai (the Lord). "The LORD said unto my Lord, Sit thou at my right hand, until I make thine enemies thy footstool" (Ps. 110:1). Verses 34-35:

> 34 **For David is not ascended into the heavens: but he saith himself, The LORD said unto my Lord, Sit thou on my right hand, 35 Until I make thy foes thy footstool.**

Peter comes to his conclusion. He wants them

to know exactly what they have done! Hold up for a moment. Pay particular attention to whom he addresses his words. Verse36:

> 36 Therefore <u>let all the house of Israel know</u> assuredly, that God hath made that same Jesus, <u>whom ye have crucified</u>, both Lord and Christ.

Jesus is both God's Son and their Messiah! This same Jesus, they crucified! Look at their reaction. Verse 37:

> 37 Now when they heard this, they were pricked in their heart, and said unto Peter and to the rest of the apostles, <u>Men and brethren, what shall we do?</u>

Hearing this, they were convicted by their conscience and asked, "What shall we do?" The answer to this question is important. Peter is about to tell them what they must "do" to be saved according to the Gospel of the Kingdom.

How did Peter answer the Jews? Verse 38:

> 38 Then Peter said unto them, <u>Repent, and be baptized every one of you in</u>

the name of Jesus Christ for the remission of sins, and ye shall receive the gift of the Holy Ghost.

They must start by repenting or turning from their sin. Next, they must be baptized in the name of Jesus Christ. If they "do" this, then their sins will be in "remission." The word "remission" means their sins will be temporarily "suspended." Hold up, cowboy! Don't you mean forgiven? Here, we need to stop for a moment to consider this.

As we continue with the Book of Acts, we will begin to see a clear delineation between Jews and Gentiles, or non-Jews. When cancer is in remission, it is still present but no longer growing or getting worse. This is the case with the believing Jews. By believing and being baptized, their sins are in remission. Their sins are not yet forgiven, but they will be! Their Messiah will forgive their sins when He returns. In the meantime, those who are to be saved by the Gospel of the Kingdom must persevere until the end.

Consider the following two verses. Matthew 24:13-14:

13 **But he that [who] shall endure unto the end, the same shall be saved.**

14 And this **gospel of the kingdom** shall be preached in all the world for a witness unto all nations; and then shall the end come.

The Apostle Paul explains to the Gentiles when the Jews' sins will be forgiven. Romans 11:26-27:

26 And so all [true] Israel shall be saved: as it is written, There shall come out of Sion the Deliverer, and shall turn away ungodliness from Jacob: 27 **For this is my covenant unto them, when I shall take away their sins.**

All "believing" or "true" Israel will have their sins forgiven by their Messiah. If they continued to demonstrate their faith and endured unto the end, then He will return for them and forgive their sins!

I would like us to confirm something. To whom Peter was speaking? Just in case there is any question, are they Jews or not? We continue with Acts 1:39-40:

39 For **the promise is unto you, and to your children,** and to all that are afar off [scattered], even as many as the Lord our God shall call. 40 And with

many other words did he testify and exhort, saying, Save yourselves from this untoward [sinful] generation.

Did you see the words "promise" and "children" above? Speaking of promises, notice what Paul writes to the Gentiles concerning the purpose of Christ's earthly ministry. Romans 15:8:

8 Now I say that Jesus Christ was a minister of the circumcision for the truth of God, <u>to confirm the promises made unto the fathers</u>:

These are the promises God made to Abraham, Isaac, Jacob, and King David! These are the promises which Jesus Christ, their Messiah, confirmed by His earthly ministry. Christ confirmed, or verified, or strengthened that what God promised "to their fathers" would be fulfilled.

Peter is speaking about Jews and their children. It is to them that these promises belong! Later, we will find out about the promises God will make to the Gentiles. Be patient. There is wonderful news coming. Whereas the Jews' salvation depended upon their faith plus works to prove their faith, the Gentiles' salvation will be based upon faith in God's Word alone.

Modern churches hold this Pentecost experience to be the example they should follow. However, as we read on, we will see this is impossible. The multitude of Jews who believed the Kingdom Gospel repented, were baptized, and obeyed the teachings of the Twelve Apostles. Verses 41-42:

> 41 **Then they that gladly received his word were baptized: and the same day there were added unto them about three thousand souls.** 42 **And they continued stedfastly in the apostles' doctrine and fellowship, and in breaking of bread, and in prayers.**

As proof of their authority from God, the Apostles performed miracles, signs, and wonders. Verse 43:

> 43 **And fear came upon every soul: and many wonders and signs were done by the apostles.**

Then, in anticipation of the imminent arrival of the Kingdom, they did something very rarely done by believers today. Verses 44-45:

> 44 **And all that believed were together, and had all things common;** 45 **And sold their possessions and goods, and**

parted them to all men, as every man had need.

Believers are often called the "church." This comes from the Greek word "ekklesia." It means "the called-out ones." They are those who were "called out" of the much larger group of non-believers. Logically speaking, the "church" would be a "subset" of a much larger set. However, some mistake one "subset" as being the same as another "subset." Is it not possible to have more than one subset? Verses 46-47:

> 46 And they, <u>continuing daily with one accord in the temple</u>, and breaking bread from house to house, did eat their meat with gladness and singleness of heart,
>
> 47 Praising God, and having favour with all the people. And the Lord added to the church daily such as should be saved.

These Kingdom Believers continued daily at the temple awaiting the arrival of both the promised Kingdom and their promised King!

4

Acts 3

At the end of Acts 2, we found the Kingdom Believers continued to meet together daily in the temple. In this chapter, Peter and John are going together to the temple one afternoon. Acts 3:1:

> 1 **Now Peter and John went up together into the temple at the hour of prayer, being the ninth hour.**

There, at the entrance, they encountered a disabled person. Verses 2-5:

> 2 **And a certain man lame from his mother's womb was carried, whom they laid daily at the gate of the temple which is called Beautiful, to ask alms of them that entered into the temple;**

3 Who [when] seeing Peter and John about to go into the temple asked an alms. 4 And Peter, fastening his eyes upon him with John, said, Look on [at] us. 5 And he gave heed [paid attention] unto them, expecting to receive something of them.

In the following, we see the purpose of the miracles being done by the Kingdom Apostles. God needed to validate or authenticate that these men were His representatives. All this happened before the eyes of those Jews at the temple. Verses 6-8:

6 Then Peter said, Silver and gold have I none; but such as I have give I thee: In the name of Jesus Christ of Nazareth rise up and walk.

7 And he took him by the right hand, and lifted him up: and immediately his feet and ankle bones received strength.

8 And he leaping up stood, and walked, and entered with them into the temple, walking, and leaping, and praising God.

Can you imagine the spectacle! This man who was

known by all these Jews as a disabled person for life was now healed. The story continues in verses 9-11

> 9 And all the people saw him walking and praising God: 10 And they knew that it was he which sat for alms at the Beautiful gate of the temple: and they were filled with wonder and amazement at that which had happened unto him.

> 11 And as the lame man which was healed held Peter and John, all the people ran together unto them in the porch that is called Solomon's, greatly wondering.

This was similar to the signs that caused the spectacle at Pentecost. This also brought a large crowd around the Apostles. Using this opportunity, Peter speaks to the Jews. He starts by giving glory to "the God of Abraham, Isaac, and Jacob." In his speech, Peter tells the Jews exactly what they have done. Bottomline: they have denied, rejected, and killed the Holy One of God. Verses 12-16:

> 12 And when Peter saw it, he answered unto the people, Ye men of Israel, why marvel ye at this? or why look ye so

earnestly on us, as though by our own power or holiness we had made this man to walk?

13 The God of Abraham, and of Isaac, and of Jacob, the God of our fathers, hath glorified his Son Jesus; whom ye delivered up, and denied him in the presence of Pilate, when he was determined to let him go.

14 But ye denied the Holy One and the Just, and desired a murderer to be granted unto you; 15 And killed the Prince of life, whom God hath raised from the dead; whereof we are witnesses.

16 And [by] his name through faith in his name hath made this man strong, whom ye see and know: yea, the faith which is by him hath given him this perfect soundness in the presence of you all.

Below, the word "wot" means "to know" or "to be aware." Peter knows that what they did was out of ignorance because they did not know. God knew that His Son must suffer. The prophets foretold the Jews this. This Messiah suffered and died, but God raised Him from the dead! Verses 17-18:

> 17 **And now, brethren, I wot [am aware] that through ignorance ye did it, as did also your rulers.**
>
> 18 **But those things, which God before had shewed by the mouth of all his prophets, that Christ should suffer, he hath so fulfilled.**

At Pentecost, they responded and asked, ". . . Men and brethren, what shall we do?" (v. 2:37). Here, having gotten their attention, Peter moves quickly into a call to action. Remember, they are in the temple. There is a crowd gathered. Here is what they "must do." Verses 19-21:

> 19 **Repent ye therefore, and be convert-ed, <u>that your sins may be blotted out, when the times of refreshing shall come from the presence of the Lord;</u>**
>
> 20 **And he shall send Jesus Christ, which before was preached unto you:**
>
> 21 **Whom the heaven must receive until the times of restitution of all things,**

which God hath spoken by the mouth
of all his holy prophets since the world
began.

This time Peter does not mention baptism. It was a
Jewish religious ritual. He concentrates on the fact
that their sins *will be* blotted out. When? They will
be blotted out at the coming of the Lord Jesus
Christ. He is currently in heaven and will remain
there. Until when? The "times of restitution of all
things" was foretold by the prophets and occurs at
the end of Jacob's Testing — the Tribulation.

In the next verses, some explanations may
help. First, a prophet is someone who is God's
mouthpiece. He speaks not his own words, but the
words of God. Moses was Israel's prophet. Under
his leadership, Israel became a nation. God would
send another Prophet like Moses. The Jews who listen to Him will be saved and those Jews who do not
listen to Him will be destroyed. Verses 22-23:

> 22 For Moses truly said unto the fathers,
> A prophet shall the Lord your God
> raise up unto you of your brethren, like
> unto me; him shall ye hear in all things
> whatsoever he shall say unto you.
>
> 23 And it shall come to pass, that every

soul, which will not hear that prophet, shall be destroyed from among the people.

Some do not like the thought of Jesus being referred to as a prophet. However, the position of Messiah has three offices: prophet, priest, and king. It was Jesus Who said, "For I have not spoken [the words] of myself; but [the words] the Father which sent me, he gave me a commandment [instruction], what I should say, and what I should speak" (Jn. 12:49). Presently, He is a Priest interceding for true Israel. In the end, He will return to become their victorious King!

Remember, Peter is in the temple. He is speaking only to the Jews there. As directed, these Apostles continued going to the "lost sheep of the house of Israel" just as Christ had instructed them. I will keep repeating this. There is a Latin proverb which translates "repetition is the mother of learning." Matthew 10:5-7:

> **5 These twelve Jesus sent forth, and commanded them, saying, <u>Go not into the way of the Gentiles</u>, and into any city of the Samaritans enter ye not:**
>
> **6 But <u>go rather to the lost sheep of the</u>**

house of Israel. 7 **And as ye go, <u>preach,</u> <u>saying, The kingdom of heaven is at</u> <u>hand.</u>**

God used prophets to speak to the Jews. Through them, He foretold them of these days. Acts 3:24:

> 24 **Yea, and all the prophets from Sam-uel and those that follow after, as many as have spoken, have likewise foretold of these days.**

Notice the words Peter uses to begin verse 25:

> 25 **<u>Ye are the children of the prophets,</u> <u>and of the covenant which God made</u> <u>with our fathers,</u> saying unto Abraham, And in thy seed shall all the kindreds of the earth be blessed.**

Who are the children of the prophets? The Jews are the children of Abraham, Isaac, and Jacob. They are the children of the prophecies and promises. Through the offspring of Abraham "shall all the kindreds of the earth be blessed." (See Genesis 26:4.)

Speaking to the Jews, Peter makes the following statement concerning them. God first sent His Son Jesus Christ to Israel so they would turn away

46

from their sins and return to Him. Verse 26:

> **26 Unto you first God, having raised up his Son Jesus, sent him to bless you, in turning away every one of you from his iniquities.**

God wants nothing more than to have Israel return to Him. As we go forward, we will see that their rejection continues unabated.

5

Acts 4

Messengers who bring God's truth to others are often set upon by the opposition. Peter was proclaiming the Gospel of the Kingdom to the Jews who were present in the temple. His message was contrary to what the "religious establishment" wanted taught. They wanted the people to remain obedient and dependent upon them. Acts 4:1:

> 1 And as they [the Apostles] spake unto the people, [then] the priests, and the captain of the temple, and the Sadducees, came upon them,

These words accurately described what happened. The opposition "came upon them." Verses 2-4:

> 2 Being grieved that they taught the people, and preached through Jesus the

resurrection from the dead. 3 And they laid hands on [grabbed] them, and put them in hold [detained them] unto the next day: for it was now eventide [almost evening].

4 Howbeit many of them which heard the word believed; and the number of the men was about five thousand.

Wow! Can you believe that? Five thousand Jewish men believed that Jesus Christ was the Messiah and the Son of God. This crowd was worshipping at the temple. They came over to see the commotion from the disabled person's healing. Imagine a large quiet public library. Someone starts leaping about and shouting praises to God. What was the result? Many of those who heard Peter's message believed.

The Apostles were seized and held by the religious authorities until the next morning when they were brought before the rulers for questioning. Verses 5-7:

5 And it came to pass on the morrow, that their rulers, and elders, and scribes, 6 And Annas the high priest, and Caiaphas, and John, and Alexander, and as many as were of the kin-

dred of the high priest, were gathered together at Jerusalem.

7 And when they had set them in the midst, they asked, By what power, or by what name, have ye done this?

They questioned by whose authority they made their statements. Peter, once again their spokesperson, stepped forward. He was not alone. Being filled with the Spirit, he spoke boldly. Verses 8-12:

8 Then Peter, filled with the Holy Ghost, said unto them, <u>Ye rulers of the people, and elders of Israel,</u>

9 If we this day be examined of the good deed done to the impotent man [the paraplegic], by what means he is made whole; 10 Be it known unto you all, and to all the people of Israel, that by the name of Jesus Christ of Nazareth, whom ye crucified, whom God raised from the dead, even [that is to say] by him [Jesus] doth this man [the disabled person] stand here before you whole.

11 This is the stone which was set at

nought of [no value by] you builders, which is become the head of the corner.

12 Neither is there salvation in any other: for there is none other name under heaven given among men, whereby we must be saved.

Peter referred to the rulers of Israel as "the builders" in Psalms 118:22:

22 The stone which the builders refused [rejected] is become the head stone of the corner [cornerstone].

Few, other than perhaps those who had lost their minds, would speak to the rulers of Israel in such a manner. For, to them, there was no authority higher than their own. These learned men who sat in judgment observed Peter's confidence. Acts 4:13:

13 Now when they saw the boldness of Peter and John, and perceived that they were unlearned and ignorant men, they marvelled; and they took knowledge of them, that they had been with Jesus.

Peter's knowledge and demeanor far exceeded that

of a lowly fisherman. They turned their eyes to the former disabled person who, as proof, stood before them fully healed. Verses 14-15:

> 14 **And beholding the man which was healed standing with them, they could say nothing against it.** 15 **But when they had commanded them to go aside out of the council, they conferred among themselves,**

The rulers commanded that these men be removed from their presence so that they might deliberate in private. How could they prudently handle this matter? By now, everyone in Jerusalem knew about it. Verses 16-17:

> 16 **Saying, What shall we do to these men? for that indeed a notable miracle hath been done by them is manifest [made known] to all them that dwell in Jerusalem; and we cannot deny it.** 17 **But that it spread no further among the people, let us straitly threaten them, that they speak henceforth to no man in this name.**

They brought the Apostles back into the chamber. Verse 18:

18 And they called them, and commanded them not to speak at all nor teach in the name of Jesus.

The Apostles received their authority from God to preach the Gospel of the Kingdom. Now, an earthly authority of men were commanding them to no longer preach that message. They were, in fact, imposing a "gag order" to suppress the truth. Filled with the Holy Spirit, here is their response. Verses 19-20:

19 But Peter and John answered and said unto them, Whether it be right in the sight of God to hearken unto you more than unto God, judge ye. **20** For we cannot but speak the things which we have seen and heard.

As suspected, the news of the healing of the disabled person had spread across Jerusalem like wildfire. This man was a regular at the temple and known by everyone. The rulers knew this. Verses 21-22:

21 So when they had further threatened them, they let them go, finding nothing how they might punish them, because of the people: for all men glorified

God for that which was done. 22 For the man was above forty years old, on whom this miracle of healing was shewed.

We can see why the Apostles were told to wait for the Comforter. He would comfort them and also inspire them. As they departed, they remembered what Christ told them when they were together. Luke 12:11-12:

11 And when they bring you unto the synagogues, and unto magistrates, and powers, take ye no thought how or what thing ye shall answer, or what ye shall say: 12 For the Holy Ghost shall teach you in the same hour what ye ought to say.

When the rulers had released them, they were filled with joy. Christ was with them and they offered praises to God. Acts 4:23-24:

23 And being let go, they went to their own company, and reported all that the chief priests and elders had said unto them.

24 And when they heard that, they lift-

ed up their voice to God with one accord, and said, Lord, thou art God,
which hast made heaven, and earth,
and the sea, and all that in them is:

Memories of various verses written in Scripture
came to mind and flooded them with emotion. They
continue their praises. Verses 25-28:

25 Who by the mouth of thy servant
David hast said, Why did the heathen
rage, and the people imagine vain
things? 26 The kings of the earth stood
up, and the rulers were gathered together against the Lord, and against his
Christ.

27 For of a truth against thy holy child
Jesus, whom thou hast anointed, both
Herod, and Pontius Pilate, with the
Gentiles, and the people of Israel, were
gathered together, 28 For to do whatsoever thy hand and thy counsel determined before to be done.

The Apostles added their own prayers concerning the threatenings they had received. Verses
29-30:

29 And now, Lord, behold their threat-enings: and grant unto thy servants, that with all boldness they may speak thy word,

30 By stretching forth thine hand to heal; and that signs and wonders may be done by the name of thy holy child Jesus.

The Apostles learned to be dependent upon the Lord through His Spirit. As a result, there was a great manifestation of God's power. Verse 31:

31 And when they had prayed, the place was shaken where they were assem-bled together; and they were all filled with the Holy Ghost, and they spake the word of God with boldness.

Please remember, as we read this, these events pertain to the Gospel of the Kingdom given by God to the Twelve Apostles. They believed Jesus Christ was their Messiah and the Son of God. From the beginning of Israel as a nation, God used miracles, signs, and wonders to authenticate that His messages were from Him. The Jews knew this, so they were neither surprised nor afraid. Instead, they received and believed the message. As a result, the number of those following the Gospel of the Kingdom increased dramatically.

The Kingdom Believers sold their possessions and shared in common with the other believers. Verses 32-35:

> 32 And the multitude of them that believed were of one heart and of one soul: neither said any of them that ought of the things which he possessed was his own; but they had all things common.
>
> 33 And with great power gave the apostles witness of the resurrection of the Lord Jesus: and great grace was upon them all.
>
> 34 Neither was there any among them that lacked: for as many as were possessors of lands or houses sold them, and brought the prices of the things that were sold, 35 And laid them down at the apostles' feet: and distribution was made unto every man according as he had need.

Today, there are Christians who want replicate the

events and experiences of these early Kingdom Believers. They forget about this communal redistribution of wealth and the sharing of all things in common. Israel is truly a commonwealth under God. The gospel message was that the Kingdom was "at hand." They eagerly awaited its arrival and the arrival of their King.

Luke mentions Barnabas by name. He will become an important part of the story later. Being completely sold out for the Kingdom, he sold his land and gave the proceeds to the Apostles. Verse 36-37:

> 36 **And Joses, who by the apostles was surnamed Barnabas, (which is, being interpreted, The son of consolation,) a Levite, and of the country of Cyprus,**
>
> 37 **Having land, sold it, and brought the money, and laid it at the apostles' feet.**

6

Acts 5

Luke includes a story about a couple who thought they could fool God. They kept some of their money from the sale of their possessions. Representing it was all of the proceeds, they lied to the Holy Spirit. As a result, they were made an example to the others. Acts 5:1-6:

> 1 **But a certain man named Ananias, with Sapphira his wife, sold a possession,** 2 **And kept back part of the price, his wife also being privy to it, and brought a certain part, and laid it at the apostles' feet.**
>
> 3 **But Peter said, Ananias, why hath Satan filled thine heart to lie to the Holy Ghost, and to keep back part of the price of the land?** 4 **Whilst it remained,**

was it not thine own? and after it was sold, was it not in thine own power? why hast thou conceived this thing in thine heart? thou hast not lied unto men, but unto God.

5 And Ananias hearing these words fell down, and gave up the ghost: and great fear came on all them that heard these things. 6 And the young men arose, wound him up, and carried him out, and buried him.

Not only did it happen to the husband, but it also happened to his wife. Verses 7-10:

7 And it was about the space of three hours after, when his wife, not knowing what was done, came in. 8 And Peter answered unto her, Tell me whether ye sold the land for so much? And she said, Yea, for so much.

9 Then Peter said unto her, How is it that ye have agreed together to tempt [test or try] the Spirit of the Lord? behold, the feet of them which have buried thy husband are at the door, and shall carry thee out.

10 Then fell she down straightway at his feet, and yielded up the ghost: and the young men came in, and found her dead, and, carrying her forth, buried her by her husband.

From the reaction, we can see the purpose of this event was to establish fear or respect for the Holy Spirit. Verse 11:

11 And great fear came upon all the church, and upon as many as heard these things.

The Apostles continued to teach from Solomon's porch which was part of the temple. Whereas their purpose was to reach the Jews, they continued doing miracles, signs, and wonders before the people. Verses 12-13:

12 And by the hands of the apostles were many signs and wonders wrought among the people; (and they were all with one accord in Solomon's porch.

13 And of the rest durst [dared] no man join himself to them: but the people magnified them.

A key point is made here. Notice that the Jews who believed the Gospel of the Kingdom met at the temple. The reputation of the Apostles continued to grow; so did the number of followers. Verses 14-16:

14 And believers were the more added to the Lord, multitudes both of men and women.)

15 Insomuch that they brought forth the sick into the streets, and laid them on beds and couches, that at the least the shadow of Peter passing by might overshadow some of them.

16 There came also a multitude out of the cities round about unto Jerusalem, bringing sick folks, and them which were vexed with unclean spirits: and they were healed everyone.

As you can imagine, this did not go unnoticed by the religious authorities who feared losing control and their authority.

The rulers were opposing God because these men were His appointed messengers. Verses 17-18:

17 Then the high priest rose up, and all

they that were with him, (which is the sect of the Sadducees,) and were filled with indignation,

18 And laid their hands on the apostles, and put them in the common prison.

An angel came and, upon releasing them, he gave them a message from God. Verses 19-20:

19 But the angel of the Lord by night opened the prison doors, and brought them forth, and said, 20 Go, stand and speak in the temple to the people all the words of this life.

Once again, the Apostles were emboldened and followed this directive. Verses 21-23:

21 And when they heard that, they entered into the temple early in the morning, and taught. But the high priest came, and they that were with him, and called the council together, and all the senate of the children of Israel, and sent to the prison to have them brought.

22 But when the officers came, and

found them not in the prison, they returned, and told, 23 Saying, 'The prison truly found we shut with all safety, and the keepers standing without before the doors: but when we had opened, we found no man within.'

They began to fear this matter could not be contained and wondered what they could do. Verses 24-25:

24 Now when the high priest and the captain of the temple and the chief priests heard these things, they doubted of them whereunto this would grow.

25 Then came one and told them, saying, Behold, the men whom ye put in prison are standing in the temple, and teaching the people.

Imagine their surprise! The Apostles had obeyed God and not the rulers of Israel. There may be a time in our future, as believers, when we too must choose Who we will obey.

The temple officers were able to bring them peaceably before the council. These Apostles now had a following and were loved by the people. Therefore, the rulers realized that this matter must be handled judiciously. Verses 26-28:

26 Then went the captain with the officers, and brought them without violence: for they feared the people, lest they should have been stoned.

27 And when they had brought them, they set them before the council: and the high priest asked them, 28 Saying, Did not we straitly command you that ye should not teach in this name? and, behold, ye have filled Jerusalem with your doctrine, and intend to bring this man's blood upon us.

Here is Peter's answer. May it be the model by which all believers should respond. Verses 29-32:

29 Then Peter and the other apostles answered and said, We ought to obey God rather than men. 30 The God of our fathers raised up Jesus, whom ye slew and hanged on a tree.

31 Him hath God exalted with his right hand to be a Prince and a Saviour, for to

<u>give repentance to Israel, and for-giveness of sins.</u>

32 And we are his witnesses of these things; and so is also the Holy Ghost, whom God hath given to them that obey him.

Their response left the rulers momentarily speechless. There was a wise Pharisee named Gamaliel. The Jews of today still recognized him as a great teacher of the Law. He asked for the Apostles to be removed from the chamber. Then, he spoke to the council privately. Verses 33- 34:

33 When they heard that, they were cut to the heart, and took counsel to slay them.

34 Then stood there up one in the council, a Pharisee, named Gamaliel, a doctor of the law, had in reputation among all the people, and commanded to put the apostles forth a little space;

Gamaliel spoke openly to the council. He reminded them of similar rebellions in the recent past. Gamaliel is still revered by Jews today. He made a valid argument. These previous rabble-rousers were short-lived and they came to nothing. However, if this is from God, then they may be fighting against God Himself! Verses 35-39:

> 35 And said unto them, Ye men of Israel, take heed to yourselves [pay attention to] what ye intend to do as touching [concerning] these men. 36 For before these days rose up Theudas, boasting himself to be somebody; to whom a number of men, about four hundred, joined themselves: who was slain; and all, as many as obeyed him, were scattered, and brought to nought [nothing].

> 37 After this man rose up Judas of Galilee in the days of the taxing, and drew away much people after him: he also perished; and all, even as many as obeyed him, were dispersed.

> 38 And now I say unto you, Refrain from these men, and let them alone: for if this counsel or this work be of men, it will come to nought [nothing]: 39 But if it be of God, ye cannot overthrow it; lest haply [possibly] ye be found even to fight against God.

By serving their own self-interests, they were fighting against God!

Being mindful of Gamaliel's counsel, they did not put the Apostles to death. Verse 40:

> 40 **And to him they agreed: and when they had called the apostles, and beaten them, they commanded that they should not speak in the name of Jesus, and let them go.**

After being beaten, they were released. They rejoiced and considered their suffering to be an honor for Christ. Verse 41:

> 41 **And they departed from the presence of the council, rejoicing that they were counted worthy to suffer shame for his name.**

As believers, we will experience trials and tribulations because of the One in Whom we believe. We should rejoice that we too are considered worthy.

Coming to the end this chapter of Acts, let us find the answer to this question. Where did the Apostles continue to teach? Verse 42:

42 And daily in the temple, and in every house, they ceased not to teach and preach Jesus Christ.

Since much of the temple proper was restricted to Jews alone, we can safely conclude that their teaching remained exclusively to the Jews – the children of Israel. Again, the Apostles continued to teach and obey the instructions Jesus had given them at the beginning of His ministry. Matthew 10:6-7:

> **6** But go rather to <u>the lost sheep of the house of Israel</u>. **7** And as ye go, preach, saying, <u>The kingdom of heaven is at hand</u>.

Nothing has changed, the Jews must keep their faith. This will apply also during the Tribulation. In the last verse of the Gospel of Matthew, we find Jesus' parting words to His Apostles.

> **19** Go ye therefore, and teach all nations, baptizing them in the name of the Father, and of the Son, and of the Holy Ghost:
>
> **20** <u>Teaching them to observe all things whatsoever I have commanded you</u>:

and, lo, I am with you alway, <u>even unto</u> <u>the end of the world</u>. Amen.

7

Acts 6

As the number of Kingdom Believers grew, problems developed amongst members regarding the sharing of the communal provisions. The wording may seem to imply here that Gentiles were within the group. Their meeting regularly in the temple would preclude Gentiles from being part of this group. Jews came to the temple from Israel as well as throughout the Roman Empire. Acts 6:1-2:

> 1 **And in those days, when the number of the disciples was multiplied, there arose a murmuring of the Grecians against the Hebrews, because their widows were neglected in the daily ministration [sharing].**

> 2 **Then the twelve called the multitude of the disciples unto them, and said, It**

is not reason that we should leave the
word of God, and serve tables.

In order for the Apostles to concentrate on the
ministry, they appointed men from within the fellowship to handle these needs. Verses 3-4:

3 **Wherefore, brethren, look ye out
among you seven men of honest report,
full of the Holy Ghost and wisdom,
whom we may appoint over this business. 4 But we will give ourselves continually to prayer, and to the ministry
of the word.**

Including the believers in the selection process
pleased the fellowship. Luke lists those who were
chosen. Nicolas is identified as a "proselyte" which
is "a Gentile converted to Judaism." This would refute the common belief that there were Gentiles
within this group at the temple. Verse 5:

5 **And the saying pleased the whole
multitude: and they chose Stephen, a
man full of faith and of the Holy
Ghost, and Philip, and Prochorus, and
Nicanor, and Timon, and Parmenas,
and Nicolas a proselyte of Antioch:**

Although the selection process involved the fellowship, it was the Apostles who charged them with that ministry. Verses 6-8:

6 **Whom they set before the apostles: and when they had prayed, they laid their hands on them.**

7 **And the word of God increased; and the number of the disciples multiplied in Jerusalem greatly; and a great company of the priests were obedient to the faith.**

8 **And <u>Stephen, full of faith and power,</u> did great wonders and miracles among the people.**

There were many Jewish men who served at the temple in the daily operation of the sacrifices. We learn that many of these men also believed in Jesus Christ as their Messiah and the Son of God.

Below, we find their fellowship or assembly was considered a synagogue. Unlike the temple, a synagogue serves as a place where Jews are taught. There was a diversity of countries represented. This may have been the result of the Pentecost revival where that ". . . same day there were added unto them about three thousand souls" (Acts 2:41). One disciple, Stephen, was recognized as being "full of faith and power." He did "great wonders and miracles among the people." It was not long before the opposition singled him out. Some of the men from within a synagogue argued with Stephen. Verses 9-10:

> 9 Then there arose certain of the synagogue, which is called the synagogue of the Libertines, and Cyrenians, and Alexandrians, and of them of Cilicia and of Asia, disputing with Stephen.

> 10 And they were not able to resist the wisdom and the spirit by which he spake.

These men could not gain superiority over his wisdom. They "suborned" men against Stephen. The word "suborn" means "to induce someone to commit perjury." In the Jewish religion, the charge of blasphemy against God was very serious. Verses 11-12:

> 11 Then they suborned men, which said, We have heard him speak blasphemous words against Moses, and against God.

12 And they stirred up the people, and the elders, and the scribes, and came upon him, and caught him, and brought him to the council,

Stephen was falsely accused by testimonies from false witnesses. These were evil men who served the god of this world. Notice how they twist the truth. Verses 13-14:

13 And [they] set up false witnesses, which said, This man ceaseth not to speak blasphemous words against this holy place, and the law:

14 For we have heard him say, that this Jesus of Nazareth shall destroy this place, and shall change the customs which Moses delivered [to] us.

I kept the following verse separate because it will be important. Above, we were told Stephen was "full of faith and power" and "did great wonders and miracles among the people." As Stephen is standing before the council of Israel's rulers, notice Luke's comment about his face. Verse 15:

15 And all that sat in the council, looking stedfastly on him, saw his face as it

had been the face of an angel.

An "angel" is "a messenger." On Whose behalf was Stephen sent as a messenger? We will find out in the next chapter when Luke records Stephen's defense.

8

Acts 7

The scene is set. In the previous chapter, we learned that Stephen was a servant of God. He was filled with the Holy Spirit, yet he is being charged with *blasphemy* against God. Before we go further, let us understand that *blasphemy* is defined as *speaking about or against God in an impious or irreverent or negative way, speaking reproachfully of God or His Holy Spirit.*

Allow me to test your knowledge. Do you recall the one sin which Jesus said would not be forgiven? We find it in Luke 12:10:

> 10 **And whosoever shall speak a word against the Son of man, it shall be forgiven him: but unto him that blasphemeth against the Holy Ghost it shall not be forgiven.**

So, the "unforgivable sin" is blasphemy against the

Holy Spirit. This will become important. In His Sermon on the Mount, Jesus warns those who judge others.

A while ago, I was questioned by an atheist who asked me, "How can God judge those who have never heard the gospel?" Many who share the gospel are also asked this question. The answer stems back to the Age of Conscience. God built into each human the knowledge of right and wrong. All of us have a conscience. Those who never hear the gospel, still have to answer for their conscience. How can this possible be fair? They will actually be judged by how their conscience judged others. They become the ones who will set the precedent by which they themselves will be judged. Here are Jesus' words in Matthew 7:1-2:

> 1 **Judge not, that ye be not judged.**
>
> 2 **For with what judgment ye judge, ye shall be judged: and with what measure ye mete [measure], it shall be measured [out] to you again.**

In the same way that non-believers judge others, according to their own consciences, they too will be judged. There is no way anyone can argue with God about that!

We are rapidly approaching a theological divergence. There will be a temporary parting of the ways between God and Israel. The Age of Law will soon be suspended or held in abeyance. God will still fulfill His promises and prophecies to Israel. However, their fulfillment will be delayed. This will happen when the rulers of Israel commit the one unforgivable sin. I will be sure you see this as it happens. Now, let us return to the narrative.

The high priest begins by asking Stephen if these charges are true. Acts 7:1:

> 1 **Then said the high priest, Are these things so?**

Stephen is being charged with a serious crime against Almighty God. This accusation is serious. If found guilty, it would lead to punishment by death. Being under the influence of the Holy Spirit, Stephen begins his defense. He recounts Israel's history to the same men who now rule it. Verses 2-5:

> 2 **And he [Stephen] said, Men, brethren, and fathers, hearken; The God of glory appeared unto our father Abraham, when he was in Mesopotamia, before he dwelt in Charran, 3 And said unto him, Get thee out of thy country,**

and from thy kindred, and come into the land which I shall shew thee.

4 Then came he [Abraham] out of the land of the Chaldaeans, and dwelt in Charran: and from thence, when his father was dead, he [God] removed him into this land, wherein ye now dwell.

5 And he [God] gave him none inheritance in it, no, not so much as to set his foot on: yet <u>he promised that he would give it to him for a possession, and to his seed after him</u>, when as yet he [Abraham] had no child.

Stephen begins with Abraham who believed God. By believing God, his faith was reckoned as righteousness. Abraham was saved by faith and, as such, is considered the father of faith. Stephen paints this picture before men who are, in fact, children of Abraham.

This history is something all Jews know since they were children, but these rulers had apparently forgotten. Standing before the highest court in Israel, he continues. Verses 6-10:

6 And God spake on this wise, That his

seed should sojourn in a strange land; and that they should bring them into bondage, and entreat them evil four hundred years.

7 And the nation [Egypt] to whom they shall be in bondage will I judge, said God: and after that shall they come forth, and serve me in this place.

8 And he [God] gave him the covenant of circumcision: and so Abraham begat Isaac, and circumcised him the eighth day; and Isaac begat Jacob; and Jacob begat the twelve patriarchs.

9 And the patriarchs, moved with envy, sold Joseph into Egypt: but God was with him, 10 And delivered him out of all his afflictions, and gave him favour and wisdom in the sight of Pharaoh king of Egypt; and he made him governor over Egypt and all his house.

Israel's patriarchs were envious of their brother Joseph and sold him into slavery. Later, by God's providence, this same brother arose to great power in Egypt.

God drove these same brothers into Egypt because of a great famine. Verses 11-18:

11 Now there came a dearth over all the land of Egypt and Chanaan, and great affliction: and our fathers found no sustenance. 12 But when Jacob heard that there was corn in Egypt, he sent out our fathers first.

13 And at the second time Joseph was made known to his brethren; and Joseph's kindred was made known unto Pharaoh. 14 Then sent Joseph, and called his father Jacob to him, and all his kindred, threescore and fifteen souls.

15 So Jacob went down into Egypt, and died, he, and our fathers, 16 And were carried over into Sychem, and laid in the sepulchre that Abraham bought for a sum of money of the sons of Emmor the father of Sychem.

17 But when the time of the promise drew nigh, which God had sworn to Abraham, the people grew and multiplied in Egypt, 18 Till another king

[Pharoah] arose, which knew not Joseph.

You can find the complete story of Joseph told in Genesis 37:2-50:26.

The children of Abraham suffered greatly under Egypt's new Pharoah and cried out to God to deliver them. Having mentioned the father of their faith, Stephen continues with the founding of their nation. Acts 7:19-25:

19 **The same [Pharoah] dealt subtilly [shrewdly] with our kindred, and evil entreated our fathers, so that they cast out their young children, to the end they might not live. 20 In which time Moses was born, and was exceeding fair, and nourished up in his father's house three months:**

21 **And when he was cast out, Pharaoh's daughter took him up, and nourished him for [as] her own son. 22 And Moses was learned in all the wisdom of the Egyptians, and was mighty in words and in deeds.**

23 **And when he [Moses] was full forty**

years old, it came into his heart to visit his brethren the children of Israel. 24 And seeing one of them suffer wrong, he defended him, and avenged him that was oppressed, and smote the Egyptian:

25 For he supposed his brethren would have understood how that God by his hand would deliver them: but they understood not.

Considering Israel's history, we find that they rarely acted in faith. They were always filled with doubt, rejection, and disbelief concerning God, their Deliverer.

Moses had interceded between two Israelite who were being abused by an Egyptian overseer. During the scuffle, the Egyptian was killed. However, these Jewish men turned against Moses whom God would appoint to save them. Verses 26-29:

26 And the next day he [Moses] shewed himself unto them as they strove, and would have set them at one again, saying, Sirs, ye are brethren; why do ye wrong one to another?

27 But he that did his neighbour wrong thrust him away, saying, <u>Who made thee a ruler and a judge over us? **28** Wilt thou kill me, as thou diddest the Egyptian yesterday?</u>

29 Then fled Moses at this saying, and was a stranger in the land of Madian, where he begat two sons.

As a result of this, Israel's deliverance was delayed another forty years as Moses fled to the wilderness.

While Moses dwelled in the wilderness, God dealt with him. The man who was once educated in Pharoah's household had now become a shepherd. How ironic! The man who dealt with sheep as a shepherd would soon be sent by God to "the lost sheep of the house of Israel" (Matt. 10:6). Moses is a "type," a "foreshadowing," or "representative" of the Savior Who would come. The Lord would be Israel's Shepherd.

Forty years more the Israelites continued to suffer. Finally, Moses returns to Egypt a different man—a man changed by God. Verses 30-34:

30 And when forty years were expired, there appeared to him in the wilderness of mount Sina an angel of the Lord in a flame of fire in a bush. 31 When Moses saw it, he wondered at the sight: and as he drew near to behold it, the voice of the Lord came unto him,

32 Saying, I am the God of thy fathers, the God of Abraham, and the God of Isaac, and the God of Jacob. Then Moses trembled, and durst [dared] not behold. 33 Then said the Lord to him, Put off thy shoes from thy feet: for the place where thou standest is holy ground.

34 I have seen, I have seen the affliction of my people which is in Egypt, and I have heard their groaning, and am come down to deliver them. And now come, I will send thee into Egypt.

Israel may have been slow to learn, but God did not forget them because of "the promises made unto the fathers" (Rom. 15:8). Verses 35-36:

35 This Moses whom they refused, saying, Who made thee a ruler and a judge? the same did God send to be a

ruler and a deliverer by the hand of the angel [messenger] which appeared to him in the bush.

36 He brought them out, after that he had shewed [them] wonders and signs in the land of Egypt, and in the Red sea, and in the wilderness forty years.

It is easy to forget that Stephen is delivering a speech before the supreme council of rulers. Filled with the Holy Spirit, he was recalling for these rulers facts every Jewish child was taught at an early age.

Stephen quotes a prophecy to the rulers. Moses had given this prophecy to Israel concerning the coming Messiah. Verse 37:

37 This is that Moses, which said unto the children of Israel, A prophet shall the Lord your God raise up unto you of [from among] your brethren, like unto me [Moses]; [and] him shall ye hear.

Moses was speaking of Jesus Christ Who would come from among His brethren. Christ was the Seed of Abraham. He was the royal Descendant of King David. Like Moses, He too would be the Prophet that God would send to Israel, but would they listen to Him?

Stephen describes Jesus as the *angel* or *messenger* that attended Israel in the Wilderness. Below, the word "church" simply means the "called-out ones" because God had separated them from all other nations. It was Christ Who was in the Wilderness with them. It was He Who was the Messenger that met with Moses face to face on Mount Sinai. Verse 38:

38 **This is he, that was in the church in the wilderness with the angel which spake to him [Moses] in the mount Sina, and with our fathers: who received the lively [living] oracles to give unto us:**

How did Israel respond to receiving the Law from Moses? Verses 39-41:

39 **To whom our fathers would not obey, but thrust him from them, and in their hearts turned back again into Egypt,**

40 **Saying unto Aaron, Make us gods to go before us: for as for this Moses,**

which brought us out of the land of Egypt, we wot [knew] not what is become of him.

41 And they made a calf in those days, and offered sacrifice unto the idol, and rejoiced in the works of their own hands.

Stephen shows that God constantly dealt with Israel's rejection. As rebellious people, He would often allow them to have their way and, as a result, they would suffer the consequences. Verses 42-43:

42 Then God turned, and gave them up to worship the host of heaven; as it is written in the book of the prophets, O ye house of Israel, have ye offered to me slain beasts and sacrifices by the space of forty years in the wilderness?

43 Yea, ye took up the tabernacle of Moloch, and the star of your god Remphan, figures which ye made to worship them: and I will carry you away beyond Babylon.

Stop for a moment to consider this. Today, are modern Christians any different from their Hebrew counterparts? The Jews had the living oracles given to them by Moses. We have the living Word of God. Yet, very few are willing to study His Word as you are studying it now. The Holy Spirit will bless you and fill you with the understanding of His Word!

While they were in the Wilderness, God gave specific instructions to Moses to build a tabernacle. This is actually a temporary dwelling place. God desired to dwell among His people. Verse 44:

> **44 Our fathers had the tabernacle of witness in the wilderness, as he had appointed, speaking unto Moses, that he should make it according to the fashion that he had seen.**

God had led Israel through the Wilderness. He had driven out the Gentiles, the non-Jews, from the Promised Land so that they could possess it. Yet, we know that it would be to these same Gentiles the Jews would give the Messiah to be killed. Verse 45:

> **45 Which also our fathers that came after brought in with Jesus into the possession of the Gentiles, whom God drave out before the face of our fathers, unto the days of David;**

He speaks about King David who wished to build a dwelling for God. However, because David was a man of war, it would be Solomon who would build His temple. Verses 46-50:

> 46 **Who found favour before God, and desired to find a tabernacle for the God of Jacob. 47 But Solomon built him an house.**

> 48 **Howbeit the most High dwelleth not in temples made with hands; as saith the prophet, 49 Heaven is my throne, and earth is my footstool: what house will ye build me? saith the Lord: or what is the place of my rest? 50 Hath not my hand made all these things?**

At this point, there is a change in Stephen's demeanor. I picture the faces of those listening to his oration to be filled with boredom and impatience. They were hard-hearted and filled with pride. Verses 51-53:

> 51 **Ye stiffnecked and uncircumcised in heart and ears, ye do always resist the Holy Ghost: as your fathers did, so do ye.**

52 Which of the prophets have not your fathers persecuted? and they have slain them which shewed before of the coming of the Just One; of whom ye have been now the betrayers and murderers:

53 [The very same] Who have received the law by the disposition of angels, and have not kept it.

There is no difference between these men and some preachers of today. They have in their possession the Word of God, but they choose to ignore it. Instead, they replace it with their own customs and traditions.

All of what Stephen said was true. They knew it and were convicted. Yet, few want to hear the truth. Frequently, when the truth is presented, it results in a backlash, often violent. Such is the case here. Verse 54:

54 When they heard these things, they were cut to the heart, and they gnashed on him with their teeth.

They were filled with an uncontrollable anger. I need you to stop for a moment. Do you remember the one sin that Christ said would not be forgiven?

It was the same sin for which Stephen was now being charged: blasphemy of the Holy Spirit. Verses 55-56:

> 55 But he [Stephen], being full of the Holy Ghost, looked up stedfastly into heaven, and saw the glory of God, and Jesus standing on the right hand of God,
>
> 56 And said, Behold, I see the heavens opened, and the Son of man <u>standing on the right hand of God</u>.

Note that Jesus, the Son of man, was no longer seated beside God. He was now standing! Many believe it was because He was prepared to return. What follows would be Israel's defining moment.

Luke records their response. Verses 57-59:

> 57 Then they cried out with a loud voice, and stopped their ears, and ran upon him with one accord, 58 And cast him out of the city, and stoned him: and <u>the witnesses laid down their clothes at a young man's feet, whose name was Saul.</u>

59 And they stoned Stephen, calling upon God, and saying, Lord Jesus, receive my spirit.

Stephen was filled with the Holy Spirit. Looking up, he saw the Risen Jesus Christ standing at the right hand of God. He asks God not to hold this against Israel. However, actions have consequences even if they are only for a season. Verse 60:

60 And he [Stephen] kneeled down, and cried with a loud voice, Lord, lay not this sin to their charge. And when he had said this, he fell asleep.

9

Acts 8

It is important we see what is happening. When we started this study of Acts, I stated that the Acts of the Apostles was a transitional book. We are about to see the beginning of that transition! Our understanding of this transition will impact our interpretation of Paul's thirteen letters that follow the book of Acts. We are moving towards the temporary suspension of the Age of Law for which Israel is the primary beneficiary. Hearing Stephen's impassioned speech, the rulers of Israel were not moved to repentance. Instead, in self-righteousness and anger, they killed someone who was filled with the Holy Spirit and speaking the truth to them. God knows how much people hate the truth. The Word of God is Truth.

At this defining moment of Israel rejection, we are introduced to someone new! This someone has never before been mentioned in the Bible. His name was Saul. Acts 8:1-2:

> 1 **And Saul was consenting unto his death. And at that time there was a great persecution against the church which was at Jerusalem; and they were all scattered abroad throughout the regions of Judaea and Samaria, except the apostles.**
>
> 2 **And devout men carried Stephen to his burial, and made great lamentation over him.**

This martyrdom of Stephen began a precarious time for the Kingdom Believers. A great persecution arose against them. The rulers of Israel continued in their anger. Many of the believers were scattered. Yet, the Apostles remained in Jerusalem in hiding.

Saul sought to apprehend these rebels who threatened the established customs and traditions of the Jewish religion. Verses 3-4:

> 3 **As for Saul, he made havock of the church, entering into every house, and haling men and women committed them to prison.**

4 Therefore they that were scattered abroad went every where preaching the word.

As they scattered, these believers continued to preach the Kingdom Gospel everywhere they went. God's messengers performed miracles, signs, and wonders to authenticate that their message was from God. Verses 5-6:

5 Then Philip went down to the city of Samaria, and preached Christ unto them.

6 And the people with one accord gave heed unto [attention to] those things which Philip spake, hearing and seeing the miracles which he did.

This caused great crowds to gather and pay attention to the message.

From the spiritual realm, the powers, principalities and rulers of darkness were being challenged. Unclean spirits were not giving up their possessions willingly. Verses 7-8:

7 For unclean spirits, crying with loud voice, came out of many that were pos-

sessed with them: and many taken with palsies, and that were lame, were healed. 8 And there was great joy in that city.

Satan counterfeits the things of God. There was a man named Simon. He saw what these believers could do in the Spirit and wanted this ability for himself. However, he was a sorcerer. Verses 9-11:

9 But there was a certain man, called Simon, which beforetime [previously] in the same city used sorcery, and bewitched the people of Samaria, giving out that [proclaiming] himself was some great one:

10 To whom they all gave heed [paid attention], from the least to the greatest, saying, This man is the great power of God. 11 And to him they had regard, because that of long time he had bewitched them with sorceries.

Philip proclaimed the Gospel of the Kingdom by baptizing believers in the name of the Father, Son, and Holy Spirit. Simon was one of them who believed and was baptized. He witnessed the miracles and signs done by Philip. Verses 12-13:

12 But when they believed Philip preaching the things concerning the kingdom of God, and the name of Jesus Christ, they were baptized, both men and women.

13 Then Simon himself believed also: and when he was baptized, he continued [along the way] with Philip, and wondered, beholding the miracles and signs which were done.

Hearing of the great work the Lord was doing in Samaria, Peter and John decided to come from Jerusalem to see for themselves. Verses 14-16:

14 Now when the apostles which were at Jerusalem heard that Samaria had received the word of God, they sent unto them Peter and John:

15 Who, when they were come down, prayed for them, that they might receive the Holy Ghost: 16 (For as yet he was fallen upon none of them: only they were baptized in the name of the Lord Jesus.)

Simon claimed to believe the Gospel of the King

dom and was baptized. He continued to shadow Philip and the apostles as they were laying hands upon other believers. He thought this skill might be useful and desired it for himself. Verses 17-19:

> 17 Then laid they their hands on them, and they received the Holy Ghost. 18 And when Simon saw that through laying on of the apostles' hands the Holy Ghost was given, he offered them money, 19 Saying, Give me also this power, that on whomsoever I lay hands, he may receive the Holy Ghost.

Here is Peter's response to Simon's request. Verses 20-24:

> 20 But Peter said unto him [Simon], Thy money perish with thee, because thou hast thought that the gift of God may be purchased with money. 21 Thou hast neither part nor lot in this matter: for thy heart is not right in the sight of God.

> 22 Repent therefore of this thy wickedness, and pray God, if perhaps the thought of thine heart may be forgiven thee. 23 For I perceive that thou art in

the gall of bitterness, and in the bond of iniquity. 24 Then answered Simon, and said, Pray ye to the Lord for me, that none of these things which ye have spoken come upon me.

Having accomplished their purpose, Peter and John returned to Jerusalem. Verse 25:

25 And they, when they had testified and preached the word of the Lord, returned to Jerusalem, and preached the gospel in many villages of the Samaritans.

The Acts of the Apostles encompasses a large span of time. The Twelve are still operating under the instructions they received from the Lord at His Ascension. All the Jews, including those who accepted and believed the Gospel of the Kingdom, were still under the Mosaic Law. Concerning the Law, Jesus was clear in Matthew 5:17-18:

17 Think not that I am come to destroy the law, or the prophets: I am not come to destroy, but [I come] to fulfil [it]. 18 For verily I say unto you, Till heaven and earth pass, one jot or one tittle shall in no wise pass from the law, till

all be fulfilled.

The Apostle Philip preached the Gospel of the Kingdom. Christ is often referred to as "the angel of the Lord." The word "angel' means "messenger." This Messenger spoke to Philip. Acts 8:26-28:

> **26 And the angel of the Lord spake unto Philip, saying, Arise, and go toward the south unto the way that goeth down from Jerusalem unto Gaza, which is desert.**
>
> **27 And he arose and went: and, behold, a man of Ethiopia, an eunuch of great authority under Candace queen of the Ethiopians, who had the charge of all her treasure, and had come to Jerusalem for to worship, 28 Was returning, and sitting in his chariot read Esaias the prophet.**

Following His instructions, Philip arrived in Gaza and heard a Gentile reading the Hebrew Scriptures. Verses 29-30:

> **29 Then the Spirit said unto Philip, Go near, and join thyself to this chariot.**

30 And Philip ran thither to him, and heard him read the prophet Esaias [Isaiah], and said, Understandest thou what thou readest? **31** And he said, <u>How can I [understand], except some man should guide me?</u> And he desired Philip that he would come up and sit with him.

The eunuch asked an intelligent question, one I wish more would ask. He wanted to know how anyone could understand Scripture without someone guiding them. You may have been taught in the past and no longer need a guide. There are many who still need a guide to help them grow in the Word of God. Those who rightly divide the Word of Truth must be able and willing to explain to those who do not understand.

The eunuch was interested enough in Scripture to be reading it. The verses he was reading were a prophecy concerning the Messiah. He was asking to understand. Verses 32-33:

32 The place of the scripture which he read was this, He was led as a sheep to the slaughter; and like a lamb dumb before his shearer, so opened he not his mouth:

33 In his humiliation his judgment was taken away: and who shall declare his generation? for his life is taken from the earth.

Here is the text he was reading. It is reassuring to know that Scripture has not changed in over two thousand years. Isaiah 53:6-7:

6 All we like sheep have gone astray; we have turned everyone to his own way; and the LORD hath laid on him the iniquity of us all.

7 He was oppressed, and he was afflicted, yet he opened not his mouth: he is brought as a lamb to the slaughter, and as a sheep before her shearers is dumb, so he openeth not his mouth.

He questions Philip about its meaning. Finding someone who wants to understand Scripture is rare. I have found most people are not interested or believe they already know everything. Acts 8:34-35:

34 And the eunuch answered Philip, and said, I pray thee, of whom speaketh the prophet this? of himself, or of some other man?

35 Then Philip opened his mouth, and began at the same scripture, and preached unto him Jesus.

The eunuch accepts and believes Philip's teaching of God's Word. Then, he asks Philip if he may be baptized. Verses 36-37:

36 And as they went on their way, they came unto a certain water: and the eunuch said, See, here is water; what doth hinder me to be baptized?

37 And Philip said, If thou believest with all thine heart, thou mayest. And he answered and said, I believe that Jesus Christ is the Son of God.

This is the hallmark of the Kingdom Believer's faith. Let us compare this to Peter's own words concerning Who Jesus Christ is. Matthew 16:15-16:

15 He [Christ] saith unto them, But whom say ye that I am? 16 And Simon Peter answered and said, [1] Thou art the Christ, [2] the Son of the living God.

Their profession of faith, under the Gospel of the

Kingdom, must be based upon Who they believe Jesus Christ to be. Their salvation comes from their belief in Who the Christ is. He is their Messiah and the Son of God. This must be followed by (1) repentance which is the turning away from one's sins, and (2) water baptism.

What are the results of their belief, repentance, and water baptism? It is the *remission* of their sins. (See Acts 2:38.) Kingdom Believers' sins are in remission until the Messiah returns and establishes His Kingdom. Then, Israel will receive forgiveness of their sins collectively as a people. (See Rom. 11:25.) We will look back at this later when we compare the Gospel of the Kingdom with the Gospel of Grace.

The eunuch was baptized into the Kingdom by Philip. Immediately, he was taken to Azotus where he continued preaching the Gospel of the Kingdom. Verses 38-40:

> 38 **And he commanded the chariot to stand still: and they went down both into the water, both Philip and the eunuch; and he baptized him.**
>
> 39 **And when they were come up out of the water, the Spirit of the Lord caught**

away Philip, that the eunuch saw him no more: and he went on his way rejoicing.

40 But Philip was found at Azotus: and passing through he preached in all the cities, till he came to Caesarea.

10

❧

Acts 9

We turn our attention to Saul also called Paul. Many Christians remember him as the person who persecuted the Kingdom Believers. This is a fact that Paul openly admits this in 1 Corinthians 15:9:

> 9 **For I [Paul] am the least of the apostles, that am not meet [worthy] to be called an apostle, <u>because I persecuted the church of God</u>.**

To their eventual consternation, many Christians hold this action against Paul. As such, they completely avoid his teaching. Later, we find out God allowed this to happen for a reason. Acts 9:1-2:

> 1 **And Saul, yet breathing out threatenings and slaughter against the disciples of the Lord, went unto the high priest,**

2 **And desired of him letters to Damascus to the synagogues, that if he found any of this way, whether they were men or women, he might bring them bound unto Jerusalem.**

He caused terror among the Kingdom Believers. The mere mention of his name brought fear and trembling. He later admits he was a mover and a shaker as he climbed his way up the ladder in the Jews' religion. Galatians 1:13-14:

13 **For ye have heard of my conversation [lifestyle] in time past in the Jews' religion, how that beyond measure I persecuted the church of God, and wasted it:**

14 **And profited [advanced] in the Jews' religion above many my equals in mine own nation, being more exceedingly zealous of the traditions of my fathers.**

Paul was a brilliant student under Gamaliel and was "more exceedingly zealous of the traditions of my fathers." He later warns believers to be careful about following the "philosophy and vain deceit, after the tradition of men, after the rudiments of the world, and not after Christ" (Col. 2:8).

Initially, it was Paul's intent to round-up these rebels and bring them back to Jerusalem to be dealt with appropriately. He began this mission on the Road to Damascus, but God intervened. Verses 3-4:

> 3 **And as he journeyed, he came near Damascus: and suddenly there shined round about him a light from heaven: 4 And he fell to the earth, and heard a voice saying unto him, Saul, Saul, why persecutest thou me?**

Imagine being on a mission to defend your religious traditions only to be confronted by God Himself. A dialogue with the Risen Savior ensues. Verse 5:

> 5 **And he [Saul] said, Who art thou, Lord? And the Lord said, I am Jesus whom thou persecutest: it is hard for thee to kick against the pricks.**

The word *prick* comes from a tool which is a stick, rod, or staff with a pointed end. Its purpose is to drive cattle in the desired direction. (Jesus has a sense of humor!) It was Paul's obstinance that brought him to this confrontation. However, he had the perfect temperament for what Christ needed him to accomplish. Up to this point, Paul was using his God-given temperament, but he was heading in the wrong direction!

Luke continues the narrative in verse 6:

6 And he [Saul] trembling and aston-ished said, Lord, what wilt thou have me to do? And the Lord said unto him, Arise, and go into the city, and it shall be told thee what thou must do.

Paul was not traveling alone. There were men with him who were witnesses. They heard the voice, but saw no one. Verses 7-9:

7 And the men which journeyed with him stood speechless, hearing a voice, but seeing no man.

8 And Saul arose from the earth; and when his eyes were opened, he saw no man: but they led him by the hand, and brought him into Damascus. 9 And he was three days without sight, and nei-ther did eat nor drink.

He reaches his destination. There, he had time to stop and reflect upon what happened. He was blind and helpless. Unable to eat or drink, he is a humbled man.

It is clear from the following text this was all part of the Lord's divine plan. God chose a man named Ananias to serve Him. Verses 10-12:

> 10 **And there was a certain disciple at Damascus, named Ananias; and to him said the Lord in a vision, Ananias. And he said, Behold, I am here, Lord.**

> 11 **And the Lord said unto him, Arise, and go into the street which is called Straight, and enquire in the house of Judas for one called Saul, of Tarsus: for, behold, he prayeth,** 12 **And hath seen in a vision a man named Ananias coming in, and putting his hand on him, that he might receive his sight.**

Saul's reputation preceded him. Ananias was aware of Saul's treachery. As such, he was hesitant to do as the Lord requested. Verses 13-14:

> 13 **Then Ananias answered, Lord, I have heard by many of this man, how much evil he hath done to thy saints at Jerusalem:**

14 And here he hath authority from the chief priests to bind all that call on thy name.

Pay attention to the Lord's reply. It discloses a critical point for our understanding. Verses 15-16:

15 But the Lord said unto him, Go thy way: <u>for he is a chosen vessel unto me, to bear my name before the Gentiles, and kings, and the children of Israel:</u>

16 For I will shew him how great things he must suffer for my name's sake.

Up to this point, the good news of salvation was directed exclusively to the "lost sheep of the house of Israel." (See Matt. 10:6.) We will see a dispensational change. The transition will be gradual, even running in tandem for a while. If God's timeline was a road, then there would be an important mile marker here.

Ananias was a faithful servant of the Lord. He obeyed the Lord's instructions. Verses 17-18:

17 And Ananias went his way, and entered into the house; and putting his hands on him said, Brother Saul, the

Lord, even Jesus, that appeared unto thee in the way as thou camest, hath sent me, that thou mightest receive thy sight, and be filled with the Holy Ghost.

18 And immediately there fell from his eyes as it had been scales: and he received sight forthwith, and arose, and was baptized.

Paul was converted by the Risen Lord Himself. He had much to learn and it will be the Lord Who will instruct him face to face. What? You might think this is a bizarre statement. Most people miss this in Paul's letter to the Corinthians. He mentions Christ's death, burial, and resurrection witnessed by people who saw Him. 1 Corinthians 15:4-8:

4 And that he was buried, and that he rose again the third day according to the scriptures:

5 And that he was seen of [1] Cephas, then of [2] the twelve: 6 After that, he was seen of [3] above five hundred brethren at once; of whom the greater part remain unto this present, but some are fallen asleep.

**7 After that, he was seen of [4] James;
then of [5] all the apostles. 8 And last of
all he was seen of [6] me also, as of one
born out of due time.**

This tells us that Paul saw the Risen Savior! Later,
we learn that Paul is taught by Christ Himself.
Many biblical scholars believe this instruction took
three years. This fact is not taught in many churches.

Following his conversion, the Kingdom Apostles and other believers accepted him. Acts 9:19:

**19 And when he had received meat
[food], he was strengthened. Then was
Saul certain days with the disciples
which were at Damascus.**

Once his health returned, he immediately began to
teach in the synagogues. Many could not believe
this was the same man. He once sought to apprehend them and bring them to judgment, but now
taught that Jesus Christ was the Son of God. This is
consistent with the Kingdom Gospel, however Paul
had not yet been schooled by the Risen Savior.
Verses 20-22:

20 And straightway he preached Christ

in the synagogues, that he is the Son of God.

21 But all that heard him were amazed, and said; Is not this he that destroyed them which called on this name in Jerusalem, and came hither for that intent, that he might bring them bound unto the chief priests?

22 But Saul increased the more in strength, and confounded the Jews which dwelt at Damascus, proving that this [Jesus] is very Christ.

Paul began his ministry by going to the Jew first. This would change later on. It was not long before the Jews who were not Kingdom Believers became angry. Like Saul once did, they feared for their customs and traditions. The Jewish leaders had a good thing going. They controlled the people through their religion. Under no circumstances did they want that to change. Their honor, power, and lucrative income was being threatened. What was their response? They want to kill Paul! Verses 23-24:

23 And after that many days were fulfilled, the Jews took counsel to kill him: 24 But their laying await was

known of Saul. And they watched the gates day and night to kill him.

The Kingdom Believers were convinced Paul's conversion was genuine. They even protected him. No doubt they had heard what God had told Ananias. Paul would be" . . . a chosen vessel unto me, to bear my name before the Gentiles, and kings, and the children of Israel" (Acts 9:15). Here, we see the Kingdom Believers saving Paul. Verses 25:

25 **Then the disciples took him by night, and let him down by the wall in a basket.**

When Paul arrived in Jerusalem, the Twelve would not meet with him. They feared he might be trying to deceive them. Barnabas, who was well-known and trusted by the other apostles, interceded on Paul's behalf. Verses 26-27:

26 **And when Saul was come to Jerusalem, he assayed [tried or attempted] to join himself to the disciples: but they were all afraid of him, and believed not that he was a disciple.**

27 **But Barnabas took him, and brought him to the apostles, and declared unto**

them how he had seen the Lord in the way, and that he had spoken to him, and how he had preached boldly at Damascus in the name of Jesus.

Years later, Paul went up to Jerusalem to meet with the Twelve again. He describes this meeting in Galatians 2:1-5:

1 Then fourteen years after I [Paul] went up again to Jerusalem with Barnabas, and took Titus with me also. 2 And I went up by revelation, and communicated unto them that gospel which I preach among the Gentiles, but privately to them which were of reputation, lest by any means I should run, or had run, in vain.

3 But neither Titus, who was with me, being a Greek, was compelled to be circumcised: 4 And that because of false brethren unawares brought in, who came in privily to spy out our liberty which we have in Christ Jesus, that they might bring us into bondage:

5 To whom we gave place by subjection, no, not for an hour; that the truth

of the gospel might continue with you.

Paul wanted the Twelve to know about the gospel message given to him by the Risen Lord. He did not want it to be confused with the Gospel of the Kingdom. Paul had received a distinct gospel for the Gentiles.

From this meeting, they came to a mutual understanding. The gospel Jesus gave to the Twelve would be carried to the circumcision or the Jews. Alternatively, the gospel given to Paul would go to the uncircumcision or the Gentiles. Verses 6-9:

> 6 **But of these who seemed to be somewhat, (whatsoever they were, it maketh no matter to me: God accepteth no man's person:) for they who seemed to be somewhat in conference added nothing to me:**

> 7 **But contrariwise, when they saw that the gospel of the uncircumcision was committed unto me, as the gospel of the circumcision was unto Peter;**

> 8 **(For he [God] that wrought effectually in Peter to the apostleship of the circumcision, the same was mighty in me**

toward the Gentiles:)

9 And when James, Cephas, and John, who seemed to be pillars, perceived the grace that was given unto me, they gave to me and Barnabas the right hands of fellowship; <u>that we should go unto the heathen [Gentiles], and they unto the circumcision [Jews]</u>.

Here we find the key to understanding the New Testament. According to the inspired Word of God, there are two separate gospels! The biblical evidence is true whether we choose to believe it or not. Likewise, whether we were taught it or not! For those who claim the Word of God as their sole authority, we must consider the biblical evidence. As we continue to examine the Book of Acts, it becomes apparent the book is transitional. It takes us "from" one and brings us "to" something else. The Gospel of the Kingdom was preached by Jesus and His Twelve Apostles. The Gospel of Grace was preached by the Apostle Paul. By the end of the book of Acts, this transition will be become self-evident.

After his first meeting with the Twelve, he remained in Jerusalem. There, he continued to speak boldly which angered some. Acts 9:28-30:

28 And he was with them coming in and going out at Jerusalem.

29 And he spake boldly in the name of the Lord Jesus, and disputed against the Grecians: but they went about to slay him. **30** Which when the brethren knew, they brought him down to Caesarea, and sent him forth to Tarsus.

Few people like it when someone challenges what they believe. This especially applies when it concerns their religious beliefs. This is so true! Paul found himself in a situation where the opposition wanted to kill him. The brethren interceded by sending him away for his safety.

There was a period of peace and growth within the Kingdom churches. Verse 31:

31 Then had the churches rest throughout all Judaea and Galilee and Samaria, and were edified; and walking in the fear of the Lord, and in the comfort of the Holy Ghost, were multiplied.

The Twelve continued with their ministry to the Circumcision. Peter journeyed through Lydda. This was a town approximately twenty-two miles north-west of Jerusalem and nine miles inland from the Mediterranean Sea. Verses 32-35:

> **32 And it came to pass, as Peter passed throughout all quarters, he came down also to the saints which dwelt at Lydda. 33 And there he found a certain man named Aeneas, which had kept his bed eight years, and was sick of the palsy.**

> **34 And Peter said unto him, Aeneas, Jesus Christ maketh thee whole: arise, and make thy bed. And he arose immediately. 35 And all that dwelt at Lydda and Saron saw him, and turned to the Lord.**

Many of the Kingdom Believers believed because they saw evidence of miracles, signs, and wonders. This was something particular to Israel as God promised them He would authenticate His prophets. This does not apply to the Gentiles of whom Paul wrote, "For we walk by faith, not by sight" (2 Cor. 5:7).

There was a neighboring town of Joppa located on the Mediterranean coast in which a woman, a Kingdom Believer, became sick and died. Hearing Peter was nearby, the Kingdom Believers sent messengers asking him to come to them. Verses 36-38:

36 Now there was at Joppa a certain disciple named Tabitha, which by interpretation is called Dorcas: this woman was full of good works and alms deeds which she did. 37 And it came to pass in those days, that she was sick, and died: whom when they had washed, they laid her in an upper chamber.

38 And forasmuch as Lydda was nigh to Joppa, and the disciples had heard that Peter was there, they sent unto him two men, desiring him that he would not delay to come to them.

These men returned to Joppa with Peter. Verses 39-42:

39 Then Peter arose and went with them. When he was come, they brought him into the upper chamber: and all the widows stood by him weeping, and shewing the coats and garments which Dorcas made, while she was with them.

40 But Peter put them all forth [out],

and kneeled down, and prayed; and turning him to the body said, Tabitha, arise. And she opened her eyes: and when she saw Peter, she sat up.

41 And he gave her his hand, and lifted her up, and when he had called the saints and widows, [he] presented her alive.

42 And it was known throughout all Joppa; and many believed in the Lord.

Of course, news of this miracle traveled quickly. Many wanted to know more about this Messiah Who was the Son of God and the Gospel of His Kingdom. For this reason, Peter decided to stay in Joppa for some time. Verse 43:

43 And it came to pass, that he tarried many days in Joppa with one Simon a tanner.

11

Acts 10

The Twelve Apostles continued their ministry to the Kingdom Believers by proclaiming the Gospel of the Kingdom. While Peter was staying in Joppa, there was a devout man in nearby Caesarea who prayed to God regularly. God needed to teach Peter something. Acts 10:1-8:

1 There was a certain man in Caesarea called Cornelius, a centurion of the band called the Italian band,

2 A devout man, and one that feared God with all his house, which gave much alms to the people, and prayed to God alway. 3 He saw in a vision evidently about the ninth hour of the day an angel of God coming in to him, and saying unto him, Cornelius.

4 And when he looked on him, he was afraid, and said, What is it, Lord? And he said unto him, Thy prayers and thine alms are come up for a memorial before God. 5 And now send men to Joppa, and call for one Simon, whose surname is Peter: 6 He lodgeth with one Simon a tanner, whose house is by the sea side: he shall tell thee what thou oughtest to do.

7 And when the angel which spake unto Cornelius was departed, he called two of his household servants, and a devout soldier of them that waited on him continually; 8 And when he had declared all these things unto them, he sent them to Joppa.

Peter was a devout Jew and followed the Law of Moses. About midday, he went to the rooftop to pray. Verses 9-13:

9 On the morrow, as they went on their journey, and drew nigh unto the city, Peter went up upon the housetop to pray about the sixth hour: 10 And he became very hungry, and would have eaten: but while they made ready, he

fell into a trance,

11 And [he] saw heaven opened, and a certain vessel descending unto him, as it had been a great sheet knit at the four corners, and let down to the earth:

12 Wherein were all manner of four-footed beasts of the earth, and wild beasts, and creeping things, and fowls of the air.

13 And there came a voice to him, Rise, Peter; kill, and eat.

Jews must follow strict dietary restrictions. This makes certain foods unacceptable or unclean. Yet, the Lord told Peter to eat what was considered unclean according to their tradition. Here is Peter's lesson. Verses 14-16:

14 But Peter said, Not so, Lord; for I have never eaten anything that is common or unclean. 15 And the voice spake unto him again the second time, What God hath cleansed, that call not thou common. 16 This was done thrice [three times]: and the vessel was received up again into heaven.

All this was done in order to prepare Peter for what would follow. The men from Cornelius would be arriving momentarily. Verses 17-18:

> **17 Now while Peter doubted in himself what this vision which he had seen should mean, behold, the men which were sent from Cornelius had made enquiry for Simon's house, and stood before the gate, 18 And called, and asked whether Simon, which was sur-named Peter, were lodged there.**

The Spirit had already informed Peter that three visitors would arrive asking to see him. He is to go with them as the Lord instructed. Verses 19-20:

> **19 While Peter thought on the vision, the Spirit said unto him, Behold, three men seek thee. 20 Arise therefore, and get thee down, and go with them, doubting nothing: for I have sent them.**

The visitors spent the night at his residence. The next morning, Peter traveled with them to Caesarea. Verses 21-23:

> **21 Then Peter went down to the men which were sent unto him from Corne-**

lius; and said, Behold, I am he whom ye seek: what is the cause wherefore ye are come?

22 And they said, Cornelius the centurion, a just man, and one that feareth God, and of good report among all the nation of the Jews, was warned from God by an holy angel to send for thee into his house, and to hear words of thee. 23 Then called he them in, and lodged them. And on the morrow Peter went away with them, and certain brethren from Joppa accompanied him.

The next day, they reached the home of Cornelius. Verses 24-25:

24 And the morrow after they entered into Caesarea. And Cornelius waited for them, and had called together his kinsmen and near friends. 25 And as Peter was coming in, Cornelius met him, and fell down at his feet, and worshipped him.

Cornelius was so overjoyed to see the Apostle Peter that he worships him. Peter immediately stops him and explains that he is just a man. Verses 26-27:

26 But Peter took him up, saying, Stand up; I myself also am a man. **27** And as he talked with him, he went in, and found many that were come together.

Peter now understood why God showed him the vision. Here he was standing in the home of a Gentile which, under Jewish Law, was not allowed! He openly explains his conundrum to his host and his guests. Verses 28-29:

28 And he said unto them, Ye know how that it is an unlawful thing for a man that is a Jew to keep company, or come unto one of another nation; but God hath shewed me that I should not call any man common or unclean.

29 Therefore came I unto you without gainsaying [argument], as soon as I was sent for: <u>I ask therefore for what intent [reason] ye have sent for me?</u>

Cornelius responds to Peter's question. He begins with the visit from an angel. Verses 30-31:

30 And Cornelius said, Four days ago I was fasting until this hour; and at the ninth hour I prayed in my house, and,

134

behold, a man stood before me in bright clothing, 31 And said, Cornelius, thy prayer is heard, and thine alms are had in remembrance in the sight of God.

This messenger told Cornelius to contact Peter and where to find him. Verse 32:

32 Send therefore to Joppa, and call hither Simon, whose surname is Peter; he is lodged in the house of one Simon a tanner by the seaside: who, when he cometh, shall speak unto thee.

He now tells Peter why he is there. Verse 33:

33 Immediately therefore I sent to [for] thee; and thou hast well done that thou art come. <u>Now therefore are we all here present before God, to hear all things that are commanded thee of God.</u>

This would be any true evangelist's dream. Imagine a group of people sending for you and eager to hear you share the Word of God!

Looking at all the people there, Peter begins. Verse 34:

34 Then Peter opened his mouth, and said, Of a truth <u>I perceive that God is no respecter of persons</u>: **35** But in every nation he that feareth him, and worketh righteousness, is accepted with him.

Let us compare this to what the Apostle Paul wrote in Romans 2:10-11:

10 But glory, honour, and peace, <u>to every man that worketh good, to the Jew first, and also to the Gentile</u>: **11** For there is no [difference with] respect of persons with God.

Both gospels were open to the Jew and Gentile. God brought the Apostle Peter to speak before Gentiles.

Surprisingly, the Gentiles were eager to hear the Gospel of the Kingdom from Peter. Acts 10:36-38:

36 The word which God sent unto the children of Israel, preaching peace by Jesus Christ: (he is Lord of all:) **37** That word, I say, ye know, which was published throughout all Judaea, and began from Galilee, after the baptism which John preached;

38 How God anointed Jesus of Nazareth with the Holy Ghost and with power: who went about doing good, and healing all that were oppressed of the devil; for God was with him.

Peter and others chosen by God were witnesses of these things. He now testified before these Gentiles that all this was true. Verses 39-41:

39 And we are witnesses of all things which he did both in the land of the Jews, and in Jerusalem; whom they slew and hanged on a tree: 40 Him God raised up the third day, and shewed him openly;

41 Not to all the people, but unto witnesses chosen before of God, even to us, who did eat and drink with him after he rose from the dead.

Generally, in Scripture, we find the word "people" refers to "the people of Israel." The word "nations" refers to the "Gentiles." But now, this has changed to "whosoever believeth in Him." Verses 42-43:

42 And he commanded us to preach unto the people, and to testify that it is he which was ordained of God to be the Judge of quick and dead.

43 To him give all the prophets witness, that through his name whosoever believeth in him shall receive remission of sins.

God will give to "whosoever believeth in Him" the gift of the Holy Spirit. This had never happened before! Those Jewish Kingdom Believers who traveled with Peter were "gob-smacked." (I love different words. This word is British slang and means "flabbergasted." Well, you get the idea.) They were speechless! Verses 44-45:

44 While Peter yet spake these words, the Holy Ghost fell on all them which heard the word.

45 And they of the circumcision which believed were astonished, as many as came with Peter, because that on the Gentiles also was poured out the gift of the Holy Ghost.

The Spirit's presence was seen. This evidence led

Peter to ask them a question about baptism. Verses 46-47:

> **46 For they heard them speak with tongues, and magnify God. Then answered Peter, 47 Can any man forbid water, that these should not be baptized, which have received the Holy Ghost as well as we?**

The commandments that the Lord Jesus Christ gave to His Apostles at His Ascension must be followed. Those who believe the Gospel of the Kingdom must repent and be baptized "in the name of the Father, and of the Son, and of the Holy Ghost" (Matt. 28:19). Verse 48:

> **48 And he [Peter} commanded them to be baptized in the name of the Lord. Then prayed they [asked] him to tarry certain days.**

They desired that Peter would remain with them for a while.

At this time, only the Gospel of the Kingdom was being preached. Those who believe Christ is the Messiah and the Son of God must repent and be baptized. Notice this. They will receive "remission of sins." (See Matt.26:28; Mk.1:4; Lk. 1:77, 3:3, 24:47; Acts 2:38, 10:43.) It is important for you to know this. The Gospel of the Kingdom, unlike the Gospel of Grace, comes with conditions. First, all Kingdom Believers must continue to follow the Mosaic Law. Throughout Israel's history, the Jews continually demonstrated serious lack of faith in God. Therefore, second, God requires works as evidence of each Kingdom Believer's faith. James confirms this. Writing to Kingdom Believers, he ties works to evidence of an active faith. James 2:20; 26:

> **20 But wilt thou know, O vain man, that <u>faith without works is dead</u>?**

> **26 For as the body without the spirit is dead, <u>so faith without works is dead</u> also.**

In addition to works as proof of their faith, third, Kingdom Believers must "endure to the end." What exactly does that mean? Christ taught His disciples about the end times. Pay attention to Christ's words concerning the Kingdom Believers who "shall be saved." Matthew 24:13-14:

> **13 But <u>he that shall endure unto the end, the same shall be saved</u>.**

14 And this gospel of the kingdom shall be preached in all the world for a witness unto all nations; and <u>then shall the end come</u>.

At that time, the Kingdom was imminent. In the gospels, Jesus said numerous times "the Kingdom is at hand." Before the King could come, there must be the seven years to determine faithful or true Israel. Believers of the Kingdom Gospel who "endure unto the end, the same shall be saved" (v. 13). However, the Tribulation and arrival of the Kingdom were delayed because of the unbelief of Israel's rulers. When exactly did this happen?

Do you remember Stephen's speech before these rulers of Israel? He referred to an event in Israel's history that also caused a delay. Moses was a "type" or representative of the Savior who would come. God chose Moses to rescue the children of Israel from Pharoah. (See Exodus 2:11-15.) Moses killed an Egyptian overseer who was beating a Hebrew worker. Later, when Moses returned to the Hebrews, he was threatened and asked, "Who made thee a prince and a judge over us?" (Ex. 2:14). This threat caused Moses to escape into the wilderness. This event delayed their rescue for another forty years. In a similar way, Israel's rulers rejected Stephen. He was also God's messenger and filled

141

with the Holy Spirit. Their response was to kill Stephen and delay the arrival of their promised King!

The Prophet Daniel receives a chronological timeline for the establishment of the promised Kingdom. (See Daniel 9.) In my book *Letters To Theophilus*, I go into a detailed explanation of this timeline and its subsequent delay. God knew Israel would reject Him. This was no surprise since God's plans are perfect. All of God's promises and prophecies to Israel are true and will come to pass. His Word remains unchangeable!

So where is the Apostle Paul? Is it surprising that Luke has said nothing about him? Where is he? In Galatians, we see that Paul is in Arabia. This is the same place where God met face to face with Moses. On Mount Sinai in Arabia, God gave Moses the Law and the Age of Law began. Paul went into Arabia. (See Galatians 1:17.) There, Paul was taught face to face by the Risen Lord. For three years during His earthly ministry, Christ taught His Twelve. For three years, Paul receives the Gospel of Grace as the Age of Grace begins.

12

Acts 11

God had made a covenant with Abraham's children. Because of this, many Jews believed they had an exclusive monopoly with God. In other words, God would make no agreements with or promises to anyone else. They are not alone. Many Christian churches think the same way. Such is the natural pride of men. Christ was sent "to confirm the promises made unto the fathers" (Rom. 15:8). Yet, they rejected and killed their Messiah and the Son of God. You can imagine the uproar as news of Gentiles receiving the Gospel of the Kingdom spread. Some of the Jews challenged Peter. Yes, God made His desire known to Peter, but rarely have the Jews approved of what God wanted. Acts 11:1-2:

1 **And the apostles and brethren that were in Judaea heard that the Gentiles had also received the word of God.**

2 And when Peter was come up to Jerusalem, they that were of the circumcision contended with him,

Arguing with Peter, they made their opinions
known. Verses 3-4:

3 Saying, Thou wentest in to men un-
circumcised, and didst eat with them. 4
But Peter rehearsed the matter from the
beginning, and expounded it by order
unto them, saying,

In response, Peter recounts the entire story to
them from the very beginning. Verses 5-12:

5 I was in the city of Joppa praying: and
in a trance I saw a vision, A certain
vessel descend, as it had been a great
sheet, let down from heaven by four
corners; and it came even to me:

6 Upon the which when I had fastened
mine eyes, I considered, and saw four-
footed beasts of the earth, and wild
beasts, and creeping things, and fowls
of the air.

7 And I heard a voice saying unto me,

Arise, Peter; slay and eat. 8 But I said, Not so, Lord: for nothing common or unclean hath at any time entered into my mouth. 9 But the voice answered me again from heaven, What God hath cleansed, that call not thou common. 10 And this was done three times: and all were drawn up again into heaven.

11 And, behold, immediately there were three men already come unto the house where I was, sent from Caesarea unto me. 12 And the Spirit bade me go with them, nothing doubting. Moreover these six brethren accompanied me, and we entered into the man's house:

Picture these men gathered around him. They listening intently to his report. Many had looks of concern. Never before were the Jews told it was acceptable to associate with Gentiles. Like Peter, at first, they found it difficult to accept. Verses 13-17:

13 And he shewed us how he had seen an angel in his house, which stood and said unto him, Send men to Joppa, and call for Simon, whose surname is Peter;

14 Who shall tell thee words, whereby

thou and all thy house shall be saved.

15 And as I began to speak, the Holy Ghost fell on them, as on us at the beginning. 16 Then remembered I the word of the Lord, how that he said, John indeed baptized with water; but ye shall be baptized with the Holy Ghost.

17 Forasmuch then as God gave them the like gift as he did unto us, who believed on the Lord Jesus Christ; what was I, that I could withstand God?

These Jewish men were believers of the Kingdom Gospel. They listened closely as Peter gave them the details. We see their response in verse 18:

18 When they heard these things, they held their peace, and glorified God, saying, Then hath God also to the Gentiles granted repentance unto life.

After Peter concluded, they glorified God! What a wonderful response. These Kingdom Believers were men of faith and willing to submit to the desires of God. This was God working in their hearts!

Once again, let us look at Christ's instructions to the Twelve in Matthew 10:5-7:

> 5 **These twelve Jesus sent forth, and commanded them, saying, Go not into the way of the Gentiles, and into any city of the Samaritans enter ye not:** 6 **But go rather to the lost sheep of the house of Israel.**
>
> 7 **And as ye go, preach, saying, The kingdom of heaven is at hand.**

This is the command they had faithfully followed, but now there was a change. God demonstrated this to the Apostle Peter. Many of the Kingdom Believers were scattered outside Jerusalem due to the persecution. They still continued preaching to Jews only. Acts 11:19:

> 19 **Now they [those believers] which were scattered abroad upon the persecution that arose about Stephen travelled as far as Phenice, and Cyprus, and Antioch, preaching the word to none but unto the Jews only.**

As the Gospel of the Kingdom spread, we can see this slowly begins to change with the help of the

Spirit. Verses 20-21:

> 20 And some of them were men of Cyprus and Cyrene, which, when they were come to Antioch, spake unto the Grecians, preaching the Lord Jesus.

> 21 And the hand of the Lord was with them: and a great number believed, and turned unto the Lord.

Barnabas was a Kingdom Believer and full of both faith and the Spirit. He was a worker who was trusted by the Apostles in Jerusalem. As such, he was dispatched to assist these new believers. Verses 22-24:

> 22 Then tidings of these things came unto the ears of the church which was in Jerusalem: and they sent forth Barnabas, that he should go as far as Antioch.

> 23 Who, when he came, and had seen the grace of God, was glad, and exhorted them all, that with purpose of heart they would cleave unto the Lord.

> 24 For he was a good man, and full of

the Holy Ghost and of faith: and much people was added unto the Lord.

This was truly an evangelism explosion. Through the preaching of the Gospel of the Kingdom, many believed, repented, and were baptized.

Barnabas leaves Antioch in search of Paul. Once he found him, he brought him back to Antioch. They remained there with the Kingdom Believers for a year. Verses 25-26:

25 Then departed Barnabas to Tarsus, for to seek Saul:

26 And when he had found him, he brought him unto Antioch. And it came to pass, that a whole year they assembled themselves with the church, and taught much people. And the disciples were called Christians first in Antioch.

A group of believers from Jerusalem arrived with news concerning a great famine. A prophet is someone who carries a message from God. One of them stands up to address the believers. Verses 27-28:

27 And in these days came prophets from Jerusalem unto Antioch.

28 And there stood up one of them named Agabus, and signified by the Spirit that there should be great dearth [famine] throughout all the world: which came to pass in the days of Claudius Caesar.

The reign of Claudius Caesar was between 41 and 54 A.D. Some time had passed since Christ's death, burial, and resurrection in 30 A.D. So, the book of Acts spans the history of His Apostles who would carry His gospels to both the Jews and the Gentiles.

Paul and Barnabas brought the alms collected from the Kingdom Believers to the elders in Jerusalem. Verses 29-30:

29 Then the disciples, every man according to his ability, determined to send relief unto the brethren which dwelt in Judaea: **30** Which also they did, and sent it to the elders [there] by the hands of Barnabas and Saul.

After his conversion, Paul was first introduced to the Apostles in Jerusalem by Barnabas who was well-known to them. Later, Paul traveled to Jerusalem with Barnabas. Galatians 2:1:

> 1 **Then fourteen years after <u>I went up again to Jerusalem with Barnabas</u>, and took Titus with me also.**

Time had passed. This important second meeting documents the distinction between the two gospels. It also records Paul's eagerness to continue supporting the needs of the Kingdom Believers in Jerusalem. Here is the conclusion of this meeting. Galatians 2:9-10:

> 9 **And when James, Cephas, and John, who seemed to be pillars, perceived the grace that was given unto me [Paul], they gave to me and Barnabas the right hands of fellowship; that [1] we should go unto the heathen [Gentiles], and [2] they unto the circumcision [Jews].**
>
> 10 **Only they would [desired] that we should remember the poor; the same which I also was [looking] forward to do.**

Paul ends by committing to support the Kingdom

Believers in Jerusalem. Later, he would bring donations collected from the assemblies of Grace Believers to Jerusalem. It would be during this future visit that Paul would be arrested. This would lead to his trial in Rome before Caesar and, ultimately, to his execution.

13

Acts 12

There is another Jewish holiday called the Feast of Unleavened Bread. This commemorates the Jews' hasty departure from Egypt. It celebrates their freedom from slavery and the beginning of their journey to the Promised Land. In the following, the word "vex" means "to irritate, make angry, plague, torment, harass, or afflict." Acts 12:1:

> 1 **Now about that time Herod the king stretched forth his hands to vex certain [leaders] of the church.**

Herod also had one of the Apostles killed which pleased the Jewish leaders. Verses 2-3:

> 2 **And he killed James the brother of John with the sword. 3 And because he saw it pleased the Jews, he proceeded**

further to take Peter also. (Then were the days of unleavened bread.)

Herod moved against Peter also, but the Lord interceded. Verses 4-5:

> 4 **And when he had apprehended him, he put him in prison, and delivered him to four quaternions of soldiers to keep him; intending after Easter to bring him forth to the people.**

> 5 **Peter therefore was kept in prison: but prayer was made without ceasing of [by] the church unto God for him.**

A "quaternion" is "a file of four Roman soldiers." Peter had sixteen guards which rotated in groups of four. It would be humanly impossible for Peter to escape unnoticed. However, it was not impossible for God Who interceded on Peter's behalf. Angels were dispatched and, once their task was complete, Peter walked out as if he was invisible. Verses 6-10:

> 6 **And when Herod would have brought him forth, the same night Peter was sleeping between two soldiers, bound with two chains: and the keepers before the door kept the prison.**

7 And, behold, the angel of the Lord came upon him, and a light shined in the prison: and he smote Peter on the side, and raised him up, saying, Arise up quickly. And his chains fell off from his hands.

8 And the angel said unto him, Gird [dress] thyself, and bind [put] on thy sandals. And so he did. And he saith unto him, Cast thy garment about thee, and follow me.

9 And he went out, and followed him; and wist not [didn't believe] that it was true which was done by the angel; but thought he saw a vision.

10 When they were past the first and the second ward, they came unto the iron gate that leadeth unto the city; which opened to them of his own accord: and they went out, and passed on through one street; and forthwith [immediately] the angel departed from him.

Peter thought it was a dream. Otherwise, he might not have handled the suspense. When Peter came to his senses, he realized what had just happened. Verse 11:

> 11 And when Peter was come to himself, he said, Now I know of a surety, [for sure] that the Lord hath sent his angel, and hath delivered me out of the hand of Herod, and from all the expectation of the people of the Jews.

Still in danger of being caught by the authorities, he made his way in darkness. He finally came to the door where the other believers were gathered. This part of the story is both humorous and so human. Verses 12-14:

> 12 And when he [Peter] had considered the thing [what happened], he came to the house of Mary the mother of John, whose surname was Mark; where many were gathered together praying.

> 13 And as Peter knocked at the door of the gate, a damsel came to hearken, named Rhoda. 14 And when she knew Peter's voice, she opened not the gate for gladness, but ran in, and told how Peter stood before the gate.

Rhoda recognized Peter's voice, but she left him standing outside. Peter continued knocking at the gate. Verses 15-16:

> 15 And they said unto her, Thou art mad. But she constantly affirmed that it was even so. Then said they, It is his angel. 16 But Peter continued knocking: and when they had opened the door, and saw him, they were astonished.

Once Peter entered the safety of the home, he motioned for them to be silent.

As they stood there astonished, he recounted the events leading up to his appearance before them. Verse 17:

> 17 But he, beckoning unto them with the hand to hold their peace, declared unto them how the Lord had brought him out of the prison. And he said, Go shew these things unto James, and to the brethren. And he departed, and went into another place.

Back at the prison, they discovered that Peter was missing. The sixteen soldiers who were charged with his custody were put to death. Verses 18-19:

18 Now as soon as it was day, there was no small stir among the soldiers, what was become of Peter.

19 And when Herod had sought for him, and found him not, he examined the keepers, and commanded that they should be put to death. And he went down from Judaea to Caesarea, and there abode.

I do not believe Herod would forget the matter of Peter. Once he was found, Herod would have put Peter to death. Let us see how God protected him.

There was a dispute involving two cities: Tyre and Sidon. These two cities were located in modern-day Lebanon along the Mediterranean coast. They were at odds with King Herod and had come to him to make peace. Verse 20:

20 And Herod was highly displeased with them [those] of Tyre and Sidon: but they came with one accord to him, and, having made Blastus the king's chamberlain their friend, [they] desired peace; because their country was nourished by the king's country.

They appeared before King Herod. They spoke platitudes praising him which he greedily accepted. Verses 21-23:

> 21 **And upon a set day Herod, arrayed in royal apparel, sat upon his throne, and [he] made an oration [speech]unto them. 22 And the people gave a shout, saying, It is the voice of a god, and not of a man.**

> 23 **And immediately the angel of the Lord smote him, because he gave not God the glory: and he was eaten of [by] worms, and gave up the ghost [died].**

Herod would have continued to vex the Kingdom Believers in order to please the Jews. Let us say, in a nutshell, God took care of the problem.

The Word of God continued to be preached and those who believed multiplied. Verse 24:

> 24 **But the word of God grew and multiplied.**

As this chapter comes to an end, we see that Paul and Barnabas returned from their trip to Jerusalem. They had completed the task of delivering the alms to the Apostles there.

> 25 **And Barnabas and Saul returned from Jerusalem, when they had fulfilled their ministry, and took with them John, whose surname was Mark.**

14

Acts 13 (Part I)

It was in Antioch that the name "Christian" was first used for believers. There is a theological heritage concerning Antioch that many Christians do not know. It has to do with writing and preservation of the New Testament manuscripts. Circumstances affect the choices people make. The persecution in Jerusalem and the great famine caused believers to scatter. They generally traveled together in groups until they found places of safety.

Many went south to Alexandria in Egypt. At that time, it was the home of the world's greatest library. It was a center of learning filled with human knowledge and Greek philosophy. Over a period of time, human knowledge began to seep into Christian doctrine. Biblical texts were being adapted with human philosophy. Scripture became corrupted. Other groups of believers left Jerusalem and traveled north to Antioch. It was here that the original biblical texts were preserved. They held to the original text. As a seminary student, I learned that from these two cities came two schools of interpretation.

The Alexandrian and Antiochian schools produced different translations. From these two translations developed different methods of interpretation. The Alexandrian school emphasized an allegorical interpretation. The Antiochian school maintained a literal interpretation. Augustine was from Alexandria. It was his allegorical theology that became the basis for the Catholic Church. Those in Antioch continued to maintain the original text and produced copies of the manuscript. These copies are considered to be the most reliable and accurate representations of the original texts. Called the Textus Receptus, it is the basis for the English Bible — the King James Bible (KJV) — published in 1611.

This chapter begins by listing some of those from the Antiochian school. Acts 13:1:

> 1 **Now there were in the church that was at Antioch certain prophets and teachers; as Barnabas, and Simeon that was called Niger, and Lucius of Cyrene, and Manaen, which had been brought up with Herod the tetrarch,**

and Saul [Paul].

Great men of the faith resided at Antioch and remained at the forefront of the Grace Gospel.

Notice that Barnabas and Paul are to be separated for the Lord's purpose. Verses 2-3:

> 2 **As they ministered to the Lord, and fasted, the Holy Ghost said, Separate me Barnabas and Saul for the work whereunto I have called them. 3 And when they had fasted and prayed, and laid their hands on them, they sent them away.**

This would be the first of three missionary trips Paul would make. He had received his teaching from the Risen Lord. Now, he was ready to begin his separate ministry. Verses 4-5:

> 4 **So they, being sent forth by the Holy Ghost, departed unto Seleucia; and from thence they sailed to Cyprus. 5 And when they were at Salamis, they preached the word of God in the synagogues of the Jews: and they had also John to their minister.**

It was Paul's custom during his early ministry to go first to the Jews. I believe he did this out of respect for the children of Abraham. On this first journey, they took with them John Mark who was mentioned earlier. (See Acts 12:25.)

During his earlier ministry, Paul performed miracles, signs, and wonders. He did this for the benefit of the Jews. Later, his ministry would move away from the Jews. When he began to concentrate on the Gentiles, these wonders would stop. He wrote these words to the Gentiles in Corinth, "For we walk by faith, not by sight" (2 Cor. 5:7). We continue with verses 6-8:

> 6 And when they had gone through the isle unto Paphos, they found a certain sorcerer, a false prophet, a Jew, whose name was Barjesus:
>
> 7 Which was with the deputy of the country, Sergius Paulus, a prudent man; who called for Barnabas and Saul, and desired to hear the word of God.
>
> 8 But Elymas the sorcerer (for so is his name by interpretation) withstood them, seeking to turn away the deputy

from the faith.

Opposition would follow Paul throughout his ministry. Verses 9-11:

9 **Then Saul, (who also is called Paul,) filled with the Holy Ghost, set his eyes on him,** 10 **And said, O full of all subtilty and all mischief, thou child of the devil, thou enemy of all righteousness, wilt thou not cease to pervert the right ways of the Lord?**

11 **And now, behold, the hand of the Lord is upon thee, and thou shalt be blind, not seeing the sun for a season. And immediately there fell on him a mist and a darkness; and he went about seeking some to lead him by the hand.**

Upon seeing this, notice the deputy's response. Verse 12:

12 **Then the deputy, when he saw what was done, believed, being astonished at the doctrine of the Lord.**

Paphos was located on the coast of the Isle of

Cyprus. From there, Paul set sail to Perga. Verse 13:

> **13 Now when Paul and his company loosed from [left] Paphos, they came to Perga in Pamphylia: and John departing from them returned to Jerusalem.**

They continued their voyage until they arrived at Perga on the coast of Asia Minor, present-day Turkey. The mission had become too much for John Mark, and he returned to Jerusalem. Paul and Barnabas would remain in Asia Minor until they returned to Antioch in Syria.

From Perga, they traveled inland to Antioch of Pisidia. Upon arriving, they went into the synagogue there. Verses 14-15:

> **14 But when they departed from Perga, they came to Antioch in Pisidia, and went into the synagogue on the sabbath day, and sat down.**
>
> **15 And after the reading of the law and the prophets the rulers of the synagogue sent unto them, saying, Ye men and brethren, if ye have any word of exhortation for the people, say on.**

While they were there, Paul was asked to speak before them. Much like Peter's speech at Pentecost, Paul's speech before the Jews recounts their history. Verses 16-26:

16 Then Paul stood up, and beckoning with his hand said, Men of Israel, and ye that fear God, give audience. 17 The God of this people of Israel chose our fathers, and exalted the people when they dwelt as strangers in the land of Egypt, and with an high arm brought he them out of it.

18 And about the time of forty years suffered he their manners in the wilderness. 19 And when he had destroyed seven nations in the land of Canaan, he divided their land to them by lot. 20 And after that he gave unto them judges about the space of four hundred and fifty years, until Samuel the prophet.

21 And afterward they desired a king: and God gave unto them Saul the son of Cis, a man of the tribe of Benjamin, by the space of forty years. 22 And when he had removed him, he raised up unto them David to be their king; to

whom also he gave testimony, and said, I have found David the son of Jesse, a man after mine own heart, which shall fulfil all my will. 23 Of this man's seed hath God according to his promise raised unto Israel a Saviour, Jesus:

24 When John [the Baptist] had first preached before his coming the baptism of repentance to all the people of Israel. 25 And as John fulfilled his course, he said, Whom think ye that I am? I am not he. But, behold, there cometh one after me, whose shoes of his feet I am not worthy to loose.

26 Men and brethren, children of the stock of Abraham, and whosoever among you feareth [respects] God, to you is the word of this salvation sent.

This was a powerful ending. Did you notice that Paul tells these Jews the Messiah and salvation through the Gospel of the Kingdom were sent to them? In Romans, he later confirms this to the Gentiles! "Now I say that Jesus Christ was a minister of the circumcision for the truth of God, to confirm the promises made unto the fathers" (Rom. 15:8).

Paul continues his speech by telling the Jews what happened to their Messiah. Verses 27-29:

27 For they that dwell at Jerusalem, and their rulers, because they knew him not, nor yet the voices of the prophets which are read every sabbath day, they have fulfilled them in condemning him. 28 And though they found no cause of death in him, yet desired they Pilate that he should be slain.

29 And when they had fulfilled all that was written of him, they took him down from the tree, and laid him in a sepulchre.

God did a miracle. Jesus had fulfilled the Law. He was a righteous Man. Therefore, death had no hold over Him. This is good news. God raised Him from the dead! Verses 30-33:

30 But God raised him from the dead: 31 And he was seen many days of them which came up with him from Galilee to Jerusalem, who are his witnesses unto the people.

32 And we declare unto you glad tid-

ings, how that <u>the promise which was made unto the fathers,</u>

33 <u>God hath fulfilled the same unto us their children,</u> in that he hath raised up Jesus again; as it is also written in the second psalm, Thou art my Son, this day have I begotten thee.

Paul later confirms Peter's words. Here is his explanation to the Gentiles believers in Rome. Romans 15:8:

8 Now I say that <u>Jesus Christ was a minister of the circumcision</u> for the truth of God, <u>to confirm the promises made unto the fathers:</u>

Paul, a Pharisee, was trained in the Law. He also knew the Writings and the Prophets. He often quoted Scripture to confirm that what happened was done by God. Acts 13:34-37:

34 And as concerning that he [God] raised him up from the dead, now no more to return to corruption, he said on this wise, I will give you the sure mercies of David.

35 Wherefore he saith also in another psalm, Thou shalt not suffer thine Holy One to see corruption.

36 For David, after he had served his own generation by the will of God, fell on sleep, and was laid unto his fathers, and saw corruption: **37** But he, whom God raised again, saw no corruption.

Having presented the facts, Paul concludes by making the following proclamation. Verse 38:

38 Be it known unto you therefore, men and brethren, that <u>through this man</u> [whom God raised again] <u>is preached unto you the forgiveness of sins</u>:

Hold up! Did Paul just say, "forgiveness of sins" here? We had better read that again to make sure he did not say "remission of sins." He definitely said, "forgiveness of sins." Therefore, Paul cannot be preaching the Gospel of the Kingdom.

When he continues, we find more evidence that this is the Gospel of Grace. Verse 39:

39 And by him [Christ] <u>all that believe are justified from all things</u>, from

which ye could not be justified by the law of Moses.

The word "justified" is an important word. It means "to be declared righteous." Paul is telling these Jews that "all" who believe or have faith in the Gospel of Grace will be "justified from all things." The words "all things" refer to "all their sins." So, by believing, all their sins will be "forgiven!" That, my friend, is definitely the Gospel of Grace!

Let us call a time-out here. I have been teaching this long enough to know that most clergy will miss this completely. So, do not feel bad. Unless you have been taught to read the Bible dispensationally and are familiar with Paul's epistles, there is no way you would have seen it. The Bible has not changed. We are still looking at the same Bible. However, it is from a dispensational perspective.

Let me show you exactly what I mean. There are so many Scriptures I could show you, but here one includes what we need. Paul is explaining the Gospel of Grace to the Gentiles. Romans 3:21-26:

> 21 **But now the righteousness of God without the law is manifested [made known], being witnessed by the law and the prophets;**

22 Even [that is to say] <u>the righteousness of God which is by faith of Jesus Christ unto all and upon all them that believe:</u> for there is no difference: 23 For all have sinned, and come short of the glory of God;

24 <u>Being justified freely by his grace [gift] through the redemption that is in Christ Jesus:</u> 25 Whom God hath set forth to be a propitiation through faith in his blood, <u>to declare his righteousness</u> for <u>the remission of sins that are past,</u> through the forbearance of God;

26 <u>To declare, I say, at this time [now] his righteousness: that he might be just [righteous], and the justifier of him which believeth in Jesus.</u>

Christ is righteous. He is the One Who is the Justifier, the One Who makes them who believe righteous. Believers are not righteous but sinners. It is through believing that we receive His righteousness. This matches with what Paul said to the Jews. His choice of words is almost identical.

There is one more Scripture to consider. It is well known by most Christians. It tells us that salvation by the Gospel of Grace is a gift. It is received through believing or having faith. Ephesians 2:8-9:

> 8 **For by grace are ye saved through faith; and that not of yourselves: it is the gift of God:** 9 **Not of works, lest any man should boast.**

Salvation through the Gospel of Grace is not something earned by works. It is not in exchange for anything we have done or will do. Otherwise, how could it be a gift from God if we have to repay it? Neither is it maintained or proven by works as the Gospel of the Kingdom requires from its believers. All that is needed for salvation through the Gospel of Grace has been paid for in full already. Through His death, burial, and resurrection, the Lord Jesus Christ paid it all!

We need to take a break. I know this chapter was long. It is unfortunate that, at this point, some readers will stop reading because this is not what they have been taught. To them I would say, "It's not what you think it says. It's not what you may want it to say. It's not what other people say it says. It is about what the Bible says."

15

Acts 13 (Part II)

High honors to those of you who continue. If you have questions, ask the Holy Spirit. Seriously! He wrote the Bible through men by *inspiration*. For anyone who truly wants to understand it, He is willing to reveal it to you by *illumination*. I constantly pray as I teach and write. Many times, I stop in the middle of something and asked the Spirit. "What does this mean?" or "How can I explain this?" If there is value in what you are reading, I cannot take the credit. It is the Comforter Who provides for our needs.

Now, let us continue with the remainder of Acts 13. Paul cautioned these Jews in the synagogue. He tells them to beware lest they fulfill the prophecies about those who choose not to believe and perish. Acts 13:40-41:

40 Beware therefore, lest that come upon you, which is spoken of in the
prophets;

41 Behold, ye despisers, and wonder,
and perish: for I work a work in your
days, a work which ye shall in no wise
believe, though a man declare it unto
you.

Paul was a Pharisee taught by Gamaliel. He knows
the history of the Jews and tells them that the promises made by God to the fathers are confirmed by
the Messiah. (See Romans 15:8.) He shares God's
gift of salvation through the Gospel of Grace. How
did they respond? Verses 42-43:

42 And when the Jews were gone out of
the synagogue, the Gentiles besought
[begged] that these words might be
preached to them the next sabbath.

43 Now when the congregation was
broken up, many of the Jews and religious proselytes followed Paul and
Barnabas: who, speaking to them, persuaded them to continue in the grace of
God.

It appears from this that many of the Jews and proselytes believed and continued in the grace of God. That means they applied the Gospel of Grace to their lives. It changed them as it removed the burden of keeping the Law as a requirement for their salvation!

The history of the Jews was recounted by Stephen before the Jerusalem council. He exposed their chronic failure in their faith towards God. Therefore, Israel can be divided into two groups: believing Israel and unbelieving Israel. Those who believe and have faith are the true children of Abraham. Those Jews who do not believe and do not have faith are not true Israel. It is for this reason the Jews must go through the Tribulation. This is why the Tribulation is called Jacob's Time of Testing. For seven years, all Israel will be tested as in a refiner's fire! Those who have faith and endure to the end will inherit the Kingdom of God. All of Christ's parables support this.

Jews theologically debate among themselves using Scripture to support their argument. It is part of their religious culture. The non-believing Jews will try to refute the believing Jews. Here is an example. Verses 44-45:

44 And the next sabbath day came almost the whole city together to hear the word of God.

45 But when the Jews saw the multitudes, they were filled with envy, and spake against those things which were spoken by Paul, contradicting and blaspheming.

Paul and Barnabas would always go to the Jews first and then to the Gentiles. Paul makes a bold proclamation to the Jews. Verses 46-47:

46 Then Paul and Barnabas waxed [grew] bold, and said, It was necessary that the word of God should first have been spoken to you [Jews]: but seeing ye put it [away] from you, and judge yourselves unworthy of everlasting life, lo, we turn to the Gentiles.

47 For so hath the Lord commanded us, saying, I have set thee to be a light of the Gentiles, that thou shouldest be for salvation unto the ends of the earth.

As God told Ananias, Paul ". . . is a chosen vessel unto me, to bear my name before the Gentiles, and kings, and the children of Israel" (Acts 9:15). Verse 48:

48 **And when the Gentiles heard this, they were glad, and glorified the word of the Lord: and as many as were ordained to eternal life believed.**

In his letter to the believers in Rome, Paul confirms his Apostleship to the Gentiles. Romans 11:13:

13 **For I speak to you Gentiles, inasmuch as I am the apostle of the Gentiles, I magnify mine office:**

During Paul's first missionary journey, this was something totally new. God knew that most Jews would lack the faith to believe. He knew they would reject the Gospel of the Kingdom offered by His Son and preached by the Twelve. Now, salvation is being offered to the Gentiles and to any Jew who will listen. This is a different gospel. This is the Gospel of Grace.

Adversity and opposition would follow them everywhere they went. As Paul and Barnabas traveled, this would not change. They said what they needed to say to those who needed to hear it. Now that it was said, they moved on. Acts 13:49-50:

49 And the word of the Lord was published [shared] throughout all the region.

50 But the Jews stirred up the devout and honourable women, and the chief men of the city, and raised persecution against Paul and Barnabas, and expelled them out of their coasts.

Above, the women there are called "honorable" which means "held in high regard, respected by or held in esteem by others." Speaking of the "chief men of the city" and the "the devout and honorable women," we are talking about influential people, the power players. They are probably religious, but are not necessarily people of faith. The Jews knew who they needed to use to achieve their intent. But, are these people really the adversaries? Paul makes it plain to the Ephesians who the true adversaries are. Ephesians 6:12:

12 For we wrestle not against flesh and blood, but against principalities, against powers, against the rulers of the darkness of this world, against spiritual wickedness in high places.

Neither Paul nor Barnabas allowed this to affect

them and moved on to the next city. Acts 13:51:

> 51 But they shook off the dust of their feet against them, and came unto Iconium. 52 And the disciples were filled with joy, and with the Holy Ghost.

They remained focused on his mission. What is that mission? Paul explains in Colossians 1:24-28:

> 24 Who now rejoice in my sufferings for you, and fill up that which is behind of the afflictions of Christ in my flesh for his body's sake, which is the church: 25 Whereof I am made a minister, according to the dispensation of God which is given to me for you [Gentiles], to fulfil the word of God;
>
> 26 Even [that is to say] the mystery which hath been hid from ages and from generations, but now is made manifest [made know] to his saints:
>
> 27 To whom God would make known what is the riches of the glory of this mystery among the Gentiles; which is Christ in you, the hope of glory:

28 [Christ] **Whom we preach, warning every man, and teaching every man in all wisdom; that we may present every man perfect in Christ Jesus:**

Later, Paul wrote to Timothy expressing God's desire that all men would come to the knowledge of His truth and choose to accept His gracious offer of salvation. 1 Timothy 2:3-4

3 For this is good and acceptable in the sight of God our Saviour; 4 Who will have all men to be saved, and to come unto the knowledge of the truth.

16

Acts 14

Paul and Barnabas continued their missionary trip to Iconium, a city in central Asia Minor. Again, they went to the Jews first. For the Jew, there is only one Temple and that is in Jerusalem. Every city with enough Jews would have a synagogue which, for them, was a place of teaching. Naturally, Paul and Barnabas started there. Acts 14:1:

> 1 **And it came to pass in Iconium, that they went both together into the synagogue of the Jews, and so spake, that a great multitude both of the Jews and also of the Greeks believed.**

From God's perspective, there are two Israels. Those who believe by faith are "true" Israel and Abraham is their true father. Of the others who do not believe, Jesus said this in John 8:44:

44 Ye are of your father the devil, and the lusts of your father ye will do. He was a murderer from the beginning, and abode not in the truth, because there is no truth in him. When he speaketh a lie, he speaketh of his own: for he is a liar, and the father of it.

Soon after, we see the arrival of the opposition who serve the lord of darkness. Acts 14:2-7:

2 But the unbelieving Jews stirred up the Gentiles, and made their minds evil affected against the brethren. 3 Long time therefore abode they, speaking boldly in the Lord, which gave testimony unto the word of his grace, and granted signs and wonders to be done by their hands.

4 But the multitude of the city was divided: and part held with the Jews, and part with the apostles. 5 And when there was an assault made both of [by] the Gentiles, and also of the Jews with their rulers, to use them despitefully, and to stone them,

6 They were aware of it, and fled unto

Lystra and Derbe, cities of Lycaonia, and unto the region that lieth round about: 7 And there they preached the gospel.

Due to the opposition, they moved on to Lystra and Derbe, both in Asia Minor. On their way there, they met a disabled person. Verses 8-11:

8 And there sat a certain man at Lystra, impotent in his feet, being a cripple from his mother's womb, who never had walked: 9 The same heard Paul speak: who stedfastly beholding him, and perceiving that he had faith to be healed,

10 Said with a loud voice, Stand upright on thy feet. And he leaped and walked. 11 And when the people saw what Paul had done, they lifted up their voices, saying in the speech of Lycaonia, The gods are come down to us in the likeness of men.

These people, being heathen or Gentiles, knew nothing of the one true God. Pagan cultures most likely believed in the Greek pantheon of gods of which there were many. Seeing this miracle, they applied their limited knowledge and decided Barnabas and Paul were gods. Verses 12-13:

> 12 **And they called Barnabas, Jupiter; and Paul, Mercurius, because he was the chief speaker.** 13 **Then the priest of Jupiter, which was before their city, brought oxen and garlands unto the gates, and would have done sacrifice with the people.**

Convinced that they were gods, the locals were determined to present them with offerings. The thought of this was appalling to both Barnabas and Paul who both protested. They began to teach them what they did not know – starting from the beginning. Verses 14-18:

> 14 **Which when the apostles, Barnabas and Paul, heard of, they rent their clothes, and ran in among the people, crying out,** 15 **And saying, Sirs, why do ye these things? We also are men of like passions with you, and preach unto you that ye should turn from these vanities unto the living God, which made heaven, and earth, and the sea, and all things that are therein:**

16 Who in times past suffered all nations to walk in their own ways. **17** Nevertheless he left not himself without witness, in that he did good, and gave us rain from heaven, and fruitful seasons, filling our hearts with food and gladness. **18** And with these sayings scarce [barely] restrained they the people, that they had not done sacrifice unto them.

Once again, the opposition appeared. This time the Jews incited the people to stone Paul. Verse 19:

19 And there came thither certain Jews from Antioch and Iconium, who persuaded the people, and, having stoned Paul, drew [dragged] him out of the city, supposing he had been dead.

What a difference: from believing they were gods to stoning them! They dragged his body to the outskirts of the city and left him there for dead. Sorrowful believers gathered around him and prayed. Miraculously, the next day Paul got up and they moved on. Verse 20:

20 Howbeit, as the disciples stood

round about him, he rose up, and came into the city [again]: and the next day he departed with Barnabas to Derbe.

Once they finished preaching the gospel in Derbe, they chose to return to the same cities that had rejected them. They wanted to meet with those who had believed and strengthen them in the faith and continue teaching them. Verses 21-22:

21 **And when they had preached the gospel to that city, and had taught many, they returned again to Lystra, and to Iconium, and Antioch, 22 Confirming the souls of the disciples, and exhorting them to continue in the faith, and that we must through much tribulation enter into the kingdom of God.**

Before they left, they appointed qualified men to the office of elder. The word "bishop" is sometimes used instead of "elder." It comes from the same Greek word "presbyteros" meaning "elder" or "senior." Their purpose was to "oversee" the brethren and not be rulers over them. Paul gives the qualifications for the offices of elder and deacon in 1 Timothy 3:1-13. Ordination is the process of conferring upon someone the office, title, and responsibilities associated with the position. Verse 23:

188

23 And when they had ordained them elders in every church [assembly], and had prayed with fasting, they commended them to the Lord, on whom they believed.

Paul and Barnabas started their return trip. As they did, they visited many of the same cities on their way back to the coast. Verses 24-25:

24 And after they had passed throughout Pisidia, they came to Pamphylia. **25** And when they had preached the word in Perga, they went down into Attalia:

Having accomplished this, they set sail back to Antioch. Verse 26:

26 And thence sailed to Antioch, from whence [where] they had been recommended to the grace of God for the work which they fulfilled.

Arriving back in Antioch, all the believers came together to hear them recount their journey. Paul and Barnabas shared their joy with the other believers and remained with them. Verses 27-28:

27 And when they were come, and had

gathered the church together, they rehearsed all that God had done with them, and how he had opened the door of faith unto the Gentiles. 28 And there they abode long time with the disciples.

The Twelve operated their ministry of the Kingdom Gospel from Jerusalem while Paul based his ministry of the Gospel of Grace from Antioch.

17

Acts 15

Paul and Barnabas were in Antioch when some of the Jews came from Jerusalem. They were wrong biblically, but that did not stop them from trying to change those who held the truth. They were taught under the Law, and rightly so. Christ came to the "Jews" with the good news of the Kingdom. He taught the "Jew" the Gospel of the Kingdom which was later rejected by their rulers

Now, God is doing something new. Paul brings good news to the "Gentiles." The Gospel of Grace is open to anyone who will listen. However, His offer of salvation as a gift received by faith will only be available for a while. God will withdraw His offer of grace at the Rapture. At that point in time, the Age of Law will resume and salvation, once again, will only be available through the Gospel of the Kingdom.

Concerning the Age of Grace and its Gospel of Grace, you might ask, "From when to when?" Paul received a different message, the Gospel of Grace. In order for Paul to be its messenger, God made him the example! God saved the "chief of sinners" by grace FIRST. So, the Age of Grace began at Paul's conversion. He was the first to be saved by grace. 1 Timothy 1:15-16:

> 15 **This is a faithful saying, and worthy of all acceptation, that <u>Christ Jesus came into the world to save sinners; of whom I am chief</u>.**

> 16 **Howbeit for this cause [reason] I obtained mercy, <u>that in me first</u> Jesus Christ might shew forth all longsuffering, for <u>a pattern to them which should hereafter believe on him to life everlasting</u>.**

The word "pattern" means "an original model or example to be copied or imitated." Here is great news. If God can save Saul, the worst of the worst, by grace, then He can save anyone!

When will the Age of Grace end? It will end at the Rapture. No longer will salvation through "faith alone" be offered. This offer will be withdrawn. All those who are "saved by grace through faith" will be removed at "His calling." This is the Rapture. Henceforth, they will remain with Him forever. Previously, we looked at a verse that showed the Jews will have their sins forgiven. Their sins are presently in remission and will be forgiven when their Messiah returns. Here is that verse again, but this time it includes the preceding verse which concerns the end of the Age of Grace. Then, the Age of Law will resume for its final seven years. At the end of the Tribulation, those Jews who believe and remain faithful will receive forgiveness. Romans 11:25:

> 25 For I [Paul] would not, brethren, that ye should be ignorant of this mystery, lest ye should be wise in your own conceits; that blindness in part is [has temporarily] happened to Israel, until the fulness of the Gentiles be come in.

Paul explains to Grace Believers that once the predetermined number of Gentiles has been saved, the Age of Grace will end. Now, what about Israel? The following applies to them and their Gospel of the Kingdom. Verses 26-27:

> 26 And so all [who are true] Israel shall be saved: as it is written, There shall

**come out of Sion the Deliverer, and
shall turn away ungodliness from Jacob:** 27 **For this is my covenant unto
them, when I shall take away their
sins.**

These well-intentioned Jews came to Antioch. They
felt obliged to teach the new believers that they
must also follow the Law. Erroneously, they believed this was a requirement of "all believers" including those saved by the Gospel of Grace.

Jerusalem's elevation is about 2500 feet above
sea level. Although Antioch is north of Jerusalem,
during their journey to Antioch they descended or
"came down" from Jerusalem. Acts 15:1:

1 **And certain men [Jews] which came
down from Judaea taught the brethren,
and said, Except ye be circumcised after the manner of Moses, ye cannot be
saved.**

However, Paul makes this clear. Grace Believers are
saved by grace which is a gift of God. They receive
salvation through faith alone which is believing
God's Word. Circumcision is a physical act. This is
something that must be "done." This makes it a
"work." Verse 2:

194

2 When therefore Paul and Barnabas had no small dissension and disputation with them [these Jews], they determined that Paul and Barnabas, and certain other of them, should go up to Jerusalem unto the apostles and elders about this question.

There was a heated discussion. Paul and Barnabas agreed to go to Jerusalem in order to settle the matter.

As they traveled to Jerusalem, they stopped and visited many of the believers' assemblies along the way. Verse 3:

3 And being brought on their way by the church [these assemblies], they passed through Phenice and Samaria, declaring the conversion of the Gentiles: and they caused great joy unto all the brethren.

There are always rumors and innuendos. The best way to announce God's decision to accept Gentiles was to be done in person by an Apostle.

The following will confirm that there are two distinct gospels. Verse 4:

4 And when they were come to Jerusalem, they were received of the church, and of the apostles and elders, and they declared all things that God had done with them.

Most Christians were never told this. So, I am down-shifting and taking this slowly. Please do not miss this since it is critical to our understanding of the New Testament. There are two gospel messages and two separate groups of recipients.

Paul writes his first epistle about this time. In it, he describes an historic meeting and assures the Grace Believers that their liberty in Christ remains secure. Here is the conclusion of this meeting. Galatians 2:1-5:

1 Then fourteen years after I went up again to Jerusalem with Barnabas, and took Titus with me also.

2 And I went up by revelation, and communicated unto them that [the] <u>gospel which I preach among the Gentiles</u>, but privately to them which were of reputation, lest by any means I should run, or had run, in vain.

3 But neither Titus, who was with me, being a Greek, was compelled to be circumcised:

4 And that because of <u>false brethren unawares brought in, who came in privily to spy out our liberty which we have in Christ Jesus, that they might bring us into bondage</u> [to the Law]:

5 To whom we gave place by subjection, no, not for an hour; that <u>the truth of the gospel</u> [of grace] might continue with you.

Paul was referring to the Jews who came to Antioch to compel believers to be circumcised according to the Law.

During the discussion at the meeting, no one added anything to what Paul had said. Verse 6:

6 But of these who seemed to be somewhat [of importance], (whatsoever they were, it maketh no matter to me: God accepteth no man's person:) for they who seemed to be somewhat in conference added nothing to me:

At this meeting, they come to an agreement which Paul outlines below. Verses 7-8:

> 7 **But contrariwise, when they saw that the gospel of the uncircumcision was committed unto me, as the gospel of the circumcision was unto Peter;**
>
> 8 **(For he that [God Who] wrought effectually in Peter to the apostleship of the circumcision, the same was mighty in me toward the Gentiles:)**

The Apostles James, Peter, and John accepted that their mission was to the Jews and Paul's mission was to the Gentiles. They showed their acceptance of this agreement by shaking hands. Verse 9:

> 9 **And when James, Cephas, and John, who seemed to be pillars, perceived the grace that was given unto me, they gave to me and Barnabas the right hands of fellowship; that we should go unto the heathen [Gentiles], and they unto the circumcision [Jews].**

These are the facts. The Bible does not change. Whether someone is taught this in their church or not, the facts are still true. You should trust the inspired Word of God and question anyone who challenges it. This information makes understanding the New Testament so much easier. So, there are two gospels. Each gospel has a specific message. Each gospel has separate and duly appointed Apostles or messengers. The Twelve take their gospel to the circumcision or Jews. Paul takes his gospel to the uncircumcision or Gentiles.

The majority of teachers and preachers will combine these two gospel messages into one! I have watched this happen many times. My friend, Les Feldick, called this "blenderized theology." They will preach the Gospel of Grace is salvation by grace through faith alone, but . . . they make "faith" into a "work." However, faith is simply "believing God." Remember this. Salvation happens the moment you believe in the finished work of Christ's death, burial, and resurrection. The requirement of "works" as "proof of faith" only applies to the Gospel of the Kingdom. Paul's words provide a perfect summary. Romans 11:6:

> 6 And **if by grace, then is it no more of works**: otherwise grace is no more grace. But **if it be of works, then is it no more grace**: otherwise work is no more work.

Returning to Acts 15, we find certain Pharisees telling Gentile believers they must complete the covenantal ritual of circumcision and they must keep the Law. Making any part of the Law a requirement for salvation would be adding works! We return to Acts 15:5:

> 5 **But there rose up certain of the sect of the Pharisees which believed, saying, That it was needful to circumcise them, and to command them to keep the law of Moses.**

In Acts 10, Cornelius and his household were Gentiles who heard Peter preach. They were saved by the Gospel of the Kingdom. Peter responds to this in verses 6-11:

> 6 **And the apostles and elders came together for to consider of this matter.**

> 7 **And when there had been much disputing, Peter rose up, and said unto them, Men and brethren, ye know how that a good while ago God made choice among us, that the Gentiles by my mouth should hear the word of the gospel, and believe.**

8 And God, which knoweth the hearts, bare them witness, giving them the Holy Ghost, even as he did unto us; 9 And put no difference between us and them, purifying their hearts by faith.

10 Now therefore why tempt ye God, to put a yoke upon the neck of the disciples, which neither our fathers nor we were able to bear? 11 But we [Jews] believe that through the grace of the Lord Jesus Christ we [Jews] shall be saved, even as they [the Gentiles].

A large group gathered to hear these men speak. Out of respect, they remained silent and listened to Paul and Barnabas. Verse 12:

12 Then all the multitude kept silence, and gave audience to Barnabas and Paul, declaring what miracles and wonders God had wrought among the Gentiles by them.

James, one of the Twelve, responds. Verses 13-18:

13 And after they [Paul and Barnabas] had held their peace [finished speaking], James answered, saying, Men and

brethren, hearken unto me: 14 Simeon hath declared how God at the first did visit the Gentiles, to take out of them a people for his name.

15 And to this agree the words of the prophets; as it is written, 16 After this I will return, and will build again the tabernacle of David, which is fallen down; and I will build again the ruins thereof, and I will set it up:

17 That the residue of men might seek after the Lord, and all the Gentiles, upon whom my name is called, saith the Lord, who doeth all these things. 18 Known unto God are all his works from the beginning of the world.

It appears that these gospels are one in the same. That is not the case. It is difficult to teach the entire New Testament in one book. It takes time. It takes patience and commitment to seek the truth. However, I must make something clear. The prophecy to which James refers is found in Amos, one of the minor prophets. It seems long, but the important verses are underlined within their context. Amos 9:11-15:

11 In that day will I raise up the tabernacle of David that is fallen, and close up the breaches thereof; and I will raise up his ruins, and I will build it as in the days of old:

12 That they may possess the remnant of Edom, and of all the heathen [Gentiles], which are called by my name, saith the LORD that doeth this.

13 Behold, the days [shall] come, saith the LORD, that the plowman shall overtake the reaper, and the treader of grapes him that soweth seed; and the mountains shall drop sweet wine, and all the hills shall melt.

14 And I will bring again the captivity of my people of Israel, and they shall build the waste cities, and inhabit them; and they shall plant vineyards, and drink the wine thereof; they shall also make gardens, and eat the fruit of them. 15 And I will plant them upon their land, and they shall no more be pulled up out of their land which I have given them, saith the LORD thy God.

Let us take a moment and look at these verses. The restoration will occur after the Rapture and at the end of the Tribulation. There were two groups of people in the Bible up until the Gospel of Grace was offered. There were Jews and there were non-Jews. But now, God has created a third group. Paul explains this to Grace Believers in Galatians 3:26-28:

> 26 **For ye are all the children of God by [through] faith in Christ Jesus. 27 For as many of you as have been [spiritually] baptized into Christ have put on Christ. 28 [Now] There is neither Jew nor Greek [Gentile], there is neither bond nor free, there is neither male nor female: for ye [as a group] are all one in Christ Jesus.**

This third entity or group is the "Body of Christ." Romans 12:4-5:

> 4 **For as we have many members in one body, and all members have not the same office:**

> 5 **So we, being many, are one body in Christ, and every one members one of another.**

The bottom line is this. We cannot and must not merge two distinct gospels or two distinct groups of people, clearly identified in Scripture, into one!

Returning to our text, I was initially surprised to find James renders the decision. It appears James had authority. Acts 15:19-21:

19 **Wherefore my sentence [determination] is, that we trouble not them, which from among the Gentiles are turned to God:**

20 **But that we write unto them, that they abstain from pollutions of idols, and from fornication, and from things strangled, and from blood.**

21 **For Moses of old time hath in every city them that preach him, being read in the synagogues every sabbath day.**

The apostles and elders in Jerusalem chose men to accompany Paul and Barnabas on their return to Antioch. They were to carry letters confirming this agreement of the Council. Verses 22-23:

22 **Then pleased it the apostles and elders, with the whole church [assem-**

bly], to send chosen men of their own company to Antioch [along] with Paul and Barnabas; namely, Judas surnamed Barsabas, and Silas, chief men among the brethren:

23 And they wrote letters by them after this manner; The apostles and elders and brethren send greeting unto the brethren which are of the Gentiles in Antioch and Syria and Cilicia:

This is exactly what Paul and Barnabas hoped to accomplish. Here is the remainder of the letter. Verses 24-29:

24 Forasmuch as we have heard, that certain [men] which went out from us have troubled you with words, subverting your souls, saying, Ye must be circumcised, and keep the law: to whom we gave no such commandment:

25 It seemed good unto us, being assembled with one accord, to send chosen men unto you [along] with our beloved Barnabas and Paul, 26 Men that have hazarded their lives for the name of our Lord Jesus Christ.

27 We have sent therefore Judas and Silas, who shall also tell you [confirm] the same things by mouth. 28 For it seemed good to the Holy Ghost, and to us, to lay upon you no greater burden than these necessary things;

29 That ye abstain from meats offered to idols, and from blood, and from things strangled, and from fornication: from which if ye keep yourselves, ye shall do well. Fare ye well.

With these letters, Paul and Barnabas were on their way along with the witnesses. Verses 30-33:

30 So when they were dismissed, they came to Antioch: and when they had gathered the multitude together, they delivered the epistle: 31 Which when they had read, they rejoiced for the consolation.

32 And Judas and Silas, being prophets also themselves, exhorted the brethren with many words, and confirmed them. 33 And after they had tarried there a space, they [these witnesses] were let go in peace from the brethren

[to return] unto the apostles [in Jerusa-lem].

However, Silas remained in Antioch with Paul and Barnabas. He would later accompany Paul on his next missionary journey. Verses 34-35:

34 Notwithstanding it pleased Silas to abide there still. 35 Paul also and Barnabas continued in Antioch, teaching and preaching the word of the Lord, with many others also.

Paul informs Barnabas it is time to return to the assemblies they established. He desired to know how these Grace Believers are faring. Verse 36:

36 And some days after Paul said unto Barnabas, Let us go again and visit our brethren in every city where we have preached the word of the Lord, and see how they do.

There arose a disagreement between Paul and Barnabas concerning John Mark. You may remember that John Mark left them before they had completed their previous missionary trip. Verses 37-38:

37 And Barnabas [was] determined to

take with them John, whose surname was Mark. 38 But Paul thought not good to take him with them, who [had] departed from them from Pamphylia, and went not with them to the work.

Paul had a powerful temperament which provided him with the necessary determination and focus for his mission. He never succumbed to the constant opposition. Once he made up his mind, it was almost impossible to change. Barnabas, being of a more congenial nature, tried unsuccessfully to change his mind. Therefore, the two parted company. Verses 39-41:

39 And the contention [disagreement] was so sharp between them, that they departed asunder one from the other: and so Barnabas took Mark, and sailed unto Cyprus;

40 And Paul chose Silas, and departed, being recommended by the brethren unto the grace of God. 41 And he went through Syria and Cilicia, confirming the churches.

We know that "all things work together for good to them that love God, to them who are the called according to his purpose" (Rom. 8:28). Here is a question. How will this disagreement work for good? Going forward, here were be two missionary teams proclaiming the Gospel of Grace!

18

Acts 16

The separation of Paul and Barnabas not only yielded two missionary teams, but it also brought Paul to Timothy. He would play an important part in helping Paul advance the Gospel of Grace. Here, Luke records their first meeting. Acts 16:1:

> 1 **Then came he [Paul] to Derbe and Lystra: and, behold, a certain disciple was there, named Timotheus, the son of a certain woman, which was a Jewess, and believed; but his father was a Greek [Gentile]:**

Timothy had a Gentile father but his mother was Jewish. He had a good reputation. Verses 2-3:

> 2 **[Timothy] Which was well reported of by the brethren that were at Lystra**

and Iconium. 3 Him would Paul have to go forth with him; and took and circumcised him because of the Jews which were in those quarters: for they knew all that his father was a Greek.

The two departed together. They brought with them the letters from the Jerusalem Council as evidence. Whether Jew or Gentile, those saved by grace were not obligated to keep the Law as a requirement for salvation. Verses 4-5:

4 And as they went through the cities, they delivered them the decrees for to keep, that were ordained of the apostles and elders which were at Jerusalem.

5 And so were the churches established in the faith, and increased in number daily.

Phrygia is located in the center of Asia Minor, present-day Turkey. (Se.) They intended to continue further north towards the Black Sea. However, the Lord directed them westward to Troas which is located on the eastern coast of the Aegean Sea. Verses 6-8:

212

6 Now when they had gone throughout Phrygia and the region of Galatia, and were forbidden of the Holy Ghost to preach the word in Asia,

7 After they were come to Mysia, they assayed [attempted] to go into Bithynia: but the Spirit suffered [allowed] them not. 8 And they passing by Mysia came down to Troas.

Paul had a dream in which a man from Macedonia requesting help appeared to him. This region is on the western coast of the Aegean Sea. Macedonia is the region north of Greece. Verses 9-10:

9 And a vision appeared to Paul in the night; There stood a man of Macedonia, and prayed [asked] him, saying, Come over into Macedonia, and help us.

10 And after he had seen the vision, immediately we endeavoured [set about] to go into Macedonia, assuredly gathering [knowing] that the Lord had called us for to preach the gospel unto them.

The word "loosing" is a nautical term. It means they "untied the lines securing the boat and set sail." Verses 11-12:

> 11 **Therefore loosing from Troas, we came with a straight course to Samothracia, and the next day to Neapolis;** 12 **And from thence to Philippi, which is the chief city of that part of Macedonia, and a colony: and we were in that city abiding certain days.**

Once they arrived in Macedonia, they remained there for a while. No doubt, they were looking for the reason why a Gentile had called them there. Verses 13-15:

> 13 **And on the sabbath we went out of the city by a river side, where prayer was wont [customarily] to be made; and we sat down, and spake unto the women which resorted thither.**

> 14 **And a certain woman named Lydia, a seller of purple, of the city of Thyatira, which worshipped God, heard us: whose heart the Lord opened, that she attended unto [listened to] the things which were spoken of Paul.**

15 And when she was baptized, and her household, she besought [begged] us, saying, If ye have judged me to be faithful to the Lord, come into my house, and abide there. And she constrained us.

Lydia was a seller of purple. Her trade was dying cloth for sale to wealthy people. No doubt, she was taking advantage of the cool along the river and using the water from the river for her trade. Listening to Paul, she would insist they stay with her.

Paul would return to teach in the shade along the river. On one occasion, they encountered a woman possessed by an evil spirit. This woman practiced divination or fortune-telling. Her owners profited from her ability. Verses 16-17:

16 And it came to pass, as we went to prayer, a certain damsel possessed with a spirit of divination met us, which brought her masters much gain by soothsaying:

17 The same followed Paul and us, and cried, saying, These men are the servants of the most high God, which shew unto us the way of salvation.

The evil spirit declared to everyone there who Paul and Barnabas were and their purpose. The opposition had arrived! She continued to annoy Paul so he dealt with the problem. As a result, the young girl was no longer vexed by this spirit. However, no longer being able to use her ability, her owners lost their income. Verses 18-19:

> 18 **And this did she many days. But Paul, being grieved, turned and said to the spirit, I command thee in the name of Jesus Christ to come out of her. And he came out the same hour.**

> 19 **And when her masters saw that the hope of their gains was gone, they caught [grabbed] Paul and Silas, and drew [pulled] them into the marketplace unto the rulers,**

Only a short time after their arrival, Paul and Silas encountered the opposition. Later, Paul would describe them as principalities, powers, and rulers of darkness. (See Ephesians 6:12.)

The Roman Empire had many religions, all of which required approval by the State. This was to assure they would not challenge the status quo. It was upon that basis they brought Paul and Barnabas before the magistrates. Verses 20-24:

20 And brought them to the magistrates, saying, These men, being Jews,
do exceedingly trouble our city, 21 And
teach customs, which are not lawful for
us to receive, neither to observe, being
Romans.

22 And the multitude rose up together
against them: and the magistrates rent
off [tore] their clothes, and commanded
to beat them.

23 And when they had laid many
stripes upon them, they cast them into
prison, charging the jailor to keep
them safely:

24 Who, having received such a charge,
thrust them into the inner prison, and
made their feet fast in the stocks.

Later, Paul may have reflected on this when
he wrote, "I have learned, in whatsoever state I am,
therewith to be content" (Phil. 4:11). For here, in the
darkness of the inner prison, they prayed and sang
praises! Verse 25:

25 And at midnight Paul and Silas prayed, and sang praises unto God: and the prisoners heard them.

That night, as God did with Peter, He would intervene on behalf of Paul. Verses 26-27:

26 And suddenly there was a great earthquake, so that the foundations of the prison were shaken: and immediately all the doors were opened, and every one's bands were loosed.

27 And the keeper of the prison awaking out of his sleep, and seeing the prison doors open, he drew out his sword, and would have killed himself, supposing that the prisoners had been fled.

Should any of the prisoners have escaped, the jailor would have been killed for breach of duty. Verses 28-29:

28 But Paul cried with a loud voice, saying, Do thyself no harm: for we are all here. **29** Then he called for a light, and sprang in, and came trembling, and fell down before Paul and Silas,

When he had brought them out from inside the prison, the jailor asked about salvation. Verses 30-34:

> 30 **And brought them out, and said, Sirs, what must I do to be saved?** 31 **And they said, Believe on the Lord Jesus Christ, and thou shalt be saved, and thy house.** 32 **And they spake unto him the word of the Lord, and to all that were in his house.**

> 33 **And he took them the same hour of the night, and washed their stripes; and was baptized, he and all his, straightway.** 34 **And when he had brought them into his house, he set meat before them, and rejoiced, believing in God with all his house.**

The Jews asked Peter the same question at Pentecost as the jailor asked. What he must "do" to be saved? Paul's response here is different. "Believe on the Lord Jesus Christ, and thou shalt be saved" (v. 31). God has "done" everything necessary for salvation by grace. There is nothing for the jailor to do, except believe. Friends, that is mental assent and not a work. He must "believe" in the Lord Jesus Christ's death, burial, and resurrection!

Since this is important, we will stop for a moment. Peter answered the Jews according to the Gospel of the Kingdom. They must (1) believe that Jesus is the Messiah and the Son of God. (2) They must repent from their sins and stop sinning. Finally, (3) they must be baptized for the *remission* of sins. Remission means "the temporary putting aside of their sins." Their sins will not be forgiven until the Messiah returns. Paul answered the jailor according to the Gospel of Grace. How does this gospel work? As sinners who were worthy of death, Christ died in our place.

Romans 6:23:

> 23 **For the wages [penalty] of sin is death; but the gift of God is eternal life through Jesus Christ our Lord.**

For the rebelliousness of sin, the righteous God requires the penalty of death. Jesus Christ took that penalty by dying on the Cross in our stead. Jesus Christ was the sinless Son of God. So, death could not hold Him because He was righteous.

Romans 4:25:

> 25 **Who was delivered for our offences,**

and was raised again for our justification.

Jesus Christ is declared by God to be righteous. It is His righteousness that He gives to those who "believe." What Jesus Christ earned, He gives freely. For that reason, Paul answered the jailor saying, "Believe on the Lord Jesus Christ, and thou shalt be saved . . ." (Acts 16:31).

The most concise statement of the Gospel of Grace was given by Paul in 1 Corinthians 15:1-4:

> 1 **Moreover, brethren, <u>I declare unto you the gospel</u> which I preached unto you, which also ye have received, and wherein ye stand;** 2 **<u>By which also ye are saved</u>, if ye keep in memory what I preached unto you, unless ye have believed in vain.** 3 **For I delivered unto you first of all that which I also received, how that [1] <u>Christ died for our sins</u> according to the scriptures;** 4 **And that [2] <u>he was buried,</u> <u>and that [3] he rose again the third day</u> according to the scriptures:**

The Gospel of Grace is based upon Christ having done it all. There is nothing for any to "do." Again, faith is not "doing" anything. It is believing! We can either choose to accept it (believe) or reject it (not believe). To this, we can add nothing.

Returning to the text, the magistrates had Paul and Barnabas flogged and thrown into prison without a trial. They did not know Paul and Silas were Roman citizens. The magistrates sent a message that they were free to go. Acts 16:35-36:

> 35 And when it was day, the magistrates sent the serjeants, saying, Let those men go. 36 And the keeper of the prison told this saying to Paul, The magistrates have sent to let you go: now therefore depart, and go in peace.

By punishing a Roman citizen without a trial, they had broken Roman law. Paul was now going to put them on the defensive. Verse 37:

> 37 But Paul said unto them, They have beaten us openly uncondemned [not convicted], being Romans [Roman citizens], and have cast us into prison; and now do they thrust us out privily [secretly]? nay verily; but let them come themselves and fetch us out.

This response was returned to the magistrates. Notice their reaction when they receive the message. Verse 38:

38 And the serjeants told these words unto the magistrates: and they feared, when they heard that they were Romans.

So, the magistrates came themselves, with fear and humility. I imagine they apologized profusely, then quickly asked them to leave their city. Verse 39:

39 And they came and besought them, and brought them out, and desired them to depart out of the city.

Paul no longer feared the magistrates, so they remained in the city long enough to visit Lydia and the other believers.

Although we are not told in the text, I picture Paul introducing the Philippian jailor and his family to the other believers in Philippi. This group of believers would grow strong in the faith and teachings of Paul. Later, we see that in the letter he wrote to the Philippians. Finishing his visit with the believers, he and Silas departed. Verse 40:

40 And they went out of the prison, and entered into the house of Lydia: and when they had seen the brethren, they comforted them, and departed.

19

Acts 17

From their successful ministry in Philippi, they followed the Via Egnatia. Similar to an interstate highway system, the Romans had a highway network connecting their vast Empire. Still in Macedonia, they arrived at Thessalonica. Acts 17:1:

> 1 Now when they had passed through Amphipolis and Apollonia, they came to Thessalonica, where was a synagogue of the Jews:

The synagogue was religious education center for the Jewish. Paul goes there first to teach anyone who would listen. He did this for three sabbaths. Verses 2-4:

> 2 And Paul, as his manner was, went in unto them [the Jews], and three sab-

bath days reasoned with them out of the scriptures,

3 Opening and alleging, that Christ must needs have suffered, and risen again from the dead; and that this Jesus, whom I preach unto you, is Christ.

4 And some of them believed, and consorted with Paul and Silas; and of the devout Greeks a great multitude, and of the chief women not a few.

The Jews who chose not to believe turned against Paul and Silas out of jealousy. The words "lewd fellows" would be "unsaved ruffians with low moral value." These Jews could have offered them money — paid protesters. Verses 5-7:

5 But the Jews which believed not, moved with envy, took unto them certain lewd fellows of the baser sort, and gathered a company, and set all the city on an uproar, and assaulted the house of Jason, and sought to bring them [Paul and Silas] out to the people.

6 And when they found them [Paul and Silas] not, they drew Jason and certain

brethren unto the rulers of the city, crying, These that have turned the world
upside down are come hither also;

7 Whom Jason hath received: and these
all do contrary to the decrees of Caesar,
saying that there is another king, one
Jesus.

This uproar evoked fear in both the people
and the leaders of the city. However, after they had
either received material or monetary guarantees as
surety, they let them go. Verses 8-9:

8 And they troubled the people and the
rulers of the city, when they heard
these things. 9 And when they had tak-
en security of Jason, and of the other,
they let them go.

As a precaution, the believers sent Paul and
Silas away for their safety. They continued in Macedonia but heading south towards Greece. They arrived in the region of Berea. As usual, their first
stop was the synagogue. Verses 10-12:

10 And the brethren immediately sent
away Paul and Silas by night unto Berea: who coming thither went into the

synagogue of the Jews.

11 These [Jews] were more noble than those in Thessalonica, in that they received the word with all readiness of mind, and searched the scriptures daily, [to see] whether those things were so.

12 Therefore many of them believed; also of honourable women which were Greeks, and of men, not a few.

Christians often emulate the Bereans because they were more noble, but why were they considered more noble? They listened to Paul teach the Word of God with an open mind. Then, they checked the Scriptures to verify whether what he said was so.

It was not long before the opposition found them. However, "we know that all things work together for good to them that love God, to them who are the called according to his purpose" (Rom. 8:28). How can this apply to this situation? Paul had preached the Gospel of Grace as the Apostle to the Gentiles. When the opposition arrived, he was forced to move on, this time by sea. Verses 13-14:

13 But when the Jews of Thessalonica

had knowledge that the word of God was preached of [by] Paul at Berea, they came thither also, and stirred up the people.

14 And then immediately the brethren sent away Paul to go as it were to the sea: but Silas and Timotheus abode there still.

Since it was Paul that they wanted, Silas and Timothy remained behind to continue building the believers in faith and sound doctrine.

When Paul arrived in Athens, he found a diverse culture of pagan religions. He sent a message back to Silas and Timothy and asked them to come to him as quickly as possible. Verse 15:

15 And they that conducted Paul brought him unto Athens: and receiving a commandment unto Silas and Timotheus for to come to him with all speed, they departed.

As he waited for them, he took the opportunity to share the gospel with Jews and Gentiles. There were also Greek philosophers from different schools of thought. Verses 16-18:

16 Now while Paul waited for them at Athens, his spirit was stirred in him, when he saw the city wholly given to idolatry. 17 Therefore disputed he in the synagogue with the Jews, and with the devout persons, and in the market daily with them that met with him.

18 Then certain philosophers of the Epicureans, and of the Stoics, encountered him. And some said, What will this babbler say? other some, He seemeth to be a setter forth of strange gods: because he preached unto them Jesus, and the resurrection.

Mars' Hill is in Athens. It is named after the Roman god of war. Its geological formation provided a slope creating a natural amphitheater. It is called the Areopagus. It held public debates, plays, and even judicial hearings. Verses 19-20:

19 And they took him [Paul], and brought him unto Areopagus, saying, May we know what this new doctrine, whereof thou speakest, is?

20 For thou bringest certain strange [new] things to our ears: we would

know therefore what these things mean.

Once could say that the general demeanor of the people could be called "curious idlers." Verse 21:

21 (For all the Athenians and strangers which were there spent their time in nothing else, but either to tell, or to hear some new thing.)

God provided him with the opportunity to speak before citizens and visitors of Athens. With excellent oratory skills, Paul begins his argument. Verses 22-23:

22 Then Paul stood in the midst of Mars' hill, and said, Ye men of Athens, I perceive that in all things ye are too superstitious. 23 For as I passed by, and beheld your devotions, I found an altar with this inscription, TO THE UN-KNOWN GOD. Whom therefore ye ignorantly worship, him declare I unto you.

When he arrived in Athens, Paul walked the streets which were filled with shrines and temples of many gods. Not wanting to leave anything to chance, the

Athenians had even created an altar to an unknown God. He continues his speech. Verses 24-29:

> 24 God that made the world and all things therein, seeing that he is Lord of heaven and earth, dwelleth not in temples made with hands; 25 Neither is worshipped with men's hands, as though he needed anything, seeing he giveth to all life, and breath, and all things; 26 And hath made of one blood all nations of men for to dwell on all the face of the earth, and hath determined the times before appointed, and the bounds of their habitation;
>
> 27 That they should seek the Lord, if haply [by chance] they might feel after him, and find him, though he be not far from every one of us: 28 For in him we live, and move, and have our being; as certain also of your own poets have said, For we are also his offspring.
>
> 29 Forasmuch then as we are the offspring of God, we ought not to think that the Godhead is like unto gold, or silver, or stone, graven by art and man's device.

He speaks about all the graven images of gold, silver, or marble that are made by the hands of man.

He tells them about times past when God overlooked men's faults and foibles. Now, God calls upon all men to repent. Verse 30:

> **30 And the times of this ignorance God winked at; <u>but now commandeth all men everywhere to repent</u>:**

There is a day of judgment coming in which all the world will be judged. He tells them about the One Who was appointed by God to judge the world. This Judge was once dead, but God raised Him from the dead. Verse 31:

> **31 Because he [God] hath appointed a day, in the which he will judge the world in righteousness by that man whom he hath ordained; whereof he hath given assurance unto all men, in that he hath raised him from the dead.**

God will judge the world in righteousness by the Righteous One Who He raised from the dead. This they can know for sure.

At the mention of the resurrection, his speech

was brought to an end. Some scoffed at the idea of a resurrection; others wanted to hear more. Verse 32:

> 32 And when they heard of the resurrection of the dead, some mocked: and others said, We will hear thee again of this matter.

When Paul departed, some stayed with him hoping to hear more. Verses 33-34:

> 33 So Paul departed from among them. 34 Howbeit certain men clave unto him, and believed: among the which was Dionysius the Areopagite, and a woman named Damaris, and others with them.

In each city where Paul preached, it is not unlike today. There are two groups: those who listened and believed and those who heard but rejected the message. Salvation in the Age of Grace is solely dependent upon each individual's faith. Believing God's Word is . . . saving faith.

20

Acts 18

Today, we would call Paul a bi-vocational preacher. He was a tentmaker and that provided for his personal needs. He did not want to be a burden to his hosts nor become indebted to anyone in the faith. The Gospel of Grace is free. Paul did not want anyone to boast that God owed them salvation because they supported His Apostle.

When Paul left Athens, he headed to Corinth which is due west. There, he met Priscilla and her husband Aquila. They would remain long-time helpers and supporters of Paul. Acts 18:1-4:

> 1 **After these things Paul departed from Athens, and came to Corinth; 2 And found a certain Jew named Aquila, born in Pontus, lately come from Italy, with his wife Priscilla; (because that**

[Emperor] Claudius had commanded all Jews to depart from Rome:) and came unto them.

3 And because he was of the same craft, he abode with them, and wrought [worked]: for by their occupation they were tentmakers. 4 And he reasoned in the synagogue every sabbath, and persuaded the Jews and the Greeks.

Once Timothy and Silas arrived, Paul grew bold to speak to the Jews. He anticipated rejection by many. It must have helped him knowing he was not alone. Verses 5-6:

5 And when Silas and Timotheus were come from Macedonia, Paul was pressed in the spirit, and testified to the Jews that Jesus was Christ.

6 And when they opposed themselves, and blasphemed, he shook his raiment, and said unto them, Your blood be upon your own heads; I am clean: from henceforth I will go unto the Gentiles.

He seem compelled to first fulfill an obligation to his own fellow countrymen. Paul writes about his

Jewish heritage in Philippians 3:5-8:

5 [I was] Circumcised the eighth day, of the stock of Israel, of the tribe of Benjamin, an Hebrew of the Hebrews; as touching the law, a Pharisee;

6 Concerning zeal, persecuting the church; touching the righteousness which is in the law, blameless. 7 But what things were gain to me, those I counted loss for Christ.

8 Yea doubtless, and I count all things but loss for the excellency of the knowledge of Christ Jesus my Lord: for whom I have suffered the loss of all things, and do count them but dung, that I may win Christ,

All these accolades he counted for dung when compared to knowing Christ! He understood the Jews. If anyone could reach them with the Gospel of Grace, it would be Paul.

Leaving the synagogue, Paul went to Justus' residence immediately adjacent to it. Verses 7-8:

7 And he departed thence, and entered

into a certain man's house, named Justus, one that worshipped God, whose house joined hard to the synagogue.

8 And Crispus, the chief ruler of the synagogue, believed on the Lord [along] with all his house; and many of the Corinthians hearing believed, and were baptized.

What a blessing to see so many believe! There was more work to be done in Corinth. God spoke to Paul in a dream. He should be bold and not fear because the Lord was with him. Verses 9-10:

9 Then spake the Lord to Paul in the night by a vision, Be not afraid, but speak, and hold not thy peace [be not silent]: 10 For I am with thee, and no man shall set on thee to hurt thee: for I have much [many] people in this city.

There were people who had heard Paul's message elsewhere and come to Corinth. We can refer to God's statement that He had many of His people in Corinth. They needed to have their faith confirmed and be taught sound doctrine. Verse 11:

11 And he continued there a year and six months, teaching the word of God among them.

Following a victory, the adversary will seek to repel their advance. Remember, God had told Paul to speak boldly saying, "for I am with thee, and no man shall set on thee to hurt thee" (v. 10). Here is the reason. Verses 12-17:

12 And when Gallio was the deputy of Achaia, the Jews made insurrection [together] with one accord against Paul, and brought him to the judgment seat, 13 Saying, This fellow persuadeth men to worship God contrary to the law.

14 And when Paul was now about to open his mouth, Gallio said unto the Jews, If it were a matter of wrong or wicked lewdness, O ye Jews, reason would that I should bear with you: 15 But if it be a question of words and names, and of your law, look ye to it [yourselves]; for I will be no judge of such matters.

16 And he [Gallio] drave [drove] them from the judgment seat. 17 Then all the

Greeks took Sosthenes, the chief ruler
of the synagogue, and beat him before
the judgment seat. And Gallio cared
for none of those things.

Gallio was truly an impartial judge. How soon do
you think these Jews will attempt this again? This
singular event allowed Paul to continue there "a
year and six months, teaching the word of God" (v.
11) in peace and safety.

He stayed in Corinth for a while. When he
was ready to move on, he took Priscilla and Aquila
with him. Verse 18:

18 And Paul after this tarried there [in
Corinth] yet a good while, and then
took his leave of the brethren, and
sailed thence [from there] into Syria,
and with him Priscilla and Aquila;
having shorn [shaved] his head in
Cenchrea: for he had a vow.

As he sailed for Syria, he was heading ultimately to
Jerusalem. Paul had made a vow or promise to the
other Twelve that he intended to fulfill. At the meeting in Jerusalem, they made one request of him. Galatians 2:10:

10 Only they would [asked] that we should remember the poor; the same which I [Paul] also was forward to do.

The poor saints in Jerusalem were suffering from both persecution and famine. Paul agreed to provide them with support.

On his voyage, he stopped at Ephesus which is located on the shore of present-day Turkey. When they arrived, he went straight to the synagogue to meet with the Jews there. Verses 19-21:

19 And he came to Ephesus, and left them there: but he himself entered into the synagogue, and reasoned with the Jews. **20** When they desired him to tarry longer time with them, he consented not;

21 But bade [wished] them farewell, saying, I must by all means keep this feast that cometh in Jerusalem: but I will return again unto you if God will [allow]. And he sailed from Ephesus.

Paul was driven to fulfill his vow. He left Priscilla and Aquila behind in Ephesus to teach the believers there. He promised that he would return.

Continuing eastward on the Mediterranean Sea, they reached the harbor in Caesarea. He greets the church there and then travels inland to Antioch in Syria. Verse 22:

22 And when he had landed at Caesarea, and gone up, and saluted the church, he went down to Antioch.

Antioch was the starting point for his two previous missionary trips. This time, Paul leaves Antioch and heads to the assemblies in Galatia and Phrygia. There, he would strengthen them in both the faith and correct doctrine. As he prepared for his trip to Jerusalem, he solicited alms for the Jewish believers there. Verse 23:

23 And after he had spent some time there [in Antioch], he departed, and went over all the country of Galatia and Phrygia in order, strengthening all the disciples.

Galatia and Phrygia are regions located in the central portion of present-day Turkey known as Asia Minor.

Paul was not the only one preaching. Barnabas and John Mark headed off to Cyprus. He left

Aquila and Priscilla behind in Ephesus to teach. While there, they met Apollos who was another preacher. Since Apollos came from Alexandria, he would have learned from the Alexandrian school. Verses 24-26:

24 **And a certain Jew named Apollos, born at Alexandria, an eloquent man, and mighty in the scriptures, came to Ephesus.**

25 **This man was instructed in the way of the Lord; and being fervent in the spirit, he spake and taught diligently the things of the Lord, knowing only the baptism of John.**

26 **And he began to speak boldly in the synagogue: whom when Aquila and Priscilla had heard, they took him [aside] unto them, and expounded unto him the way of God more perfectly.**

Providentially, Aquila and Priscilla were there and taught Apollos "the way of God more perfectly" (v. 26). Here he learned the Gospel of Grace.

Confident of what they taught him, he traveled to Achaia which is the southernmost region of

Greece. Verse 27:

> 27 And when he was disposed to pass
> into Achaia, the brethren wrote, exhort-
> ing the disciples to receive him: who,
> when he was come, helped them much
> which had believed through grace:

The believers in Ephesus had given Apollos a letter
of commendation and urged the believers in Achaia
to accept him. Verse 28:

> 28 For he mightily convinced the Jews,
> and that publicly, shewing by the
> scriptures that Jesus was Christ.

Apollos was a Jew who was well-trained in their religion. He did a wonderful job convincing the Jews
using the Scripture.

21

Acts 19

When Paul returned to Ephesus, Apollos was in Corinth in the southern part of Greece. While Paul was in Ephesus, he asked believers if they had received the Holy Spirit. Since they had been saved under the Kingdom Gospel, they had never heard of the Holy Spirit or Holy Ghost. Anyone who is saved under the Grace Gospel receives the Holy Spirit immediately upon believing. Acts 19:1-4:

> 1 And it came to pass, that, while Apollos was at Corinth, Paul having passed through the upper coasts came to Ephesus: and finding certain disciples,
>
> 2 He said unto them, Have ye received the Holy Ghost since ye believed? And they said unto him, We have not so much as heard whether there be any

Holy Ghost. 3 And he said unto them, Unto what then were ye baptized? And they said, Unto John's baptism.

4 Then said Paul, John verily baptized with the baptism of repentance, saying unto the people, that they should believe on him [the Messiah] which should come after him, that is, on Christ Jesus.

It was John the Baptist who baptized Jesus Christ to fulfill the Law. John was beheaded by Herod Antipas during Christ's earthly ministry. John called for repentance which was followed by a ritual water baptism. The Gospel of the Kingdom required belief that Jesus was the Messiah and the Son of God. Peter was the first to give a statement of faith when Christ asked. Matthew 16:15-16:

15 He [Christ] saith unto them, But whom say ye that I am? 16 And Simon Peter answered and said, <u>Thou art the Christ [Messiah], the Son of the living God</u>.

Not everyone saved by the Gospel of the Kingdom received the Holy Spirit.

Paul explained the Gospel of Grace—the finished work of Christ's death, burial, and resurrection. Those who believe immediately receive. Acts 19:5-7:

> 5 **When they heard this, they were baptized in the name of the Lord Jesus.** 6 **And when Paul had laid his hands upon them, the Holy Ghost came on them; and they spake with tongues, and prophesied.** 7 **And all the men were about twelve.**

Grace Believers receive the Holy Spirit for an important reason. Paul explains this in his wonderful letter to the Ephesians. The Holy Spirit is the earnest deposit or guaranty the believer receives the moment they believe. This "holy Spirit of Promise" assures each believer of the completion of our total redemption. They were bought by His blood and are His possession. They belong to Him. The manifestation of the Holy Spirit came upon these men with the laying on of Paul's hands. He remained in Ephesus for three months to teach them.

There is something I need to show you because it will confirm what I just told you. In his letter to the Grace Believers in Ephesus, Paul explains the role of the Holy Spirit in the redemption of a Grace Believer. Ephesians 1:12-14:

> 12 **That we should be to the praise of his glory, who first trusted in Christ.**
>
> 13 <u>**In whom ye also trusted, after that ye heard the word of truth, the gospel of your salvation: in whom also after that ye believed, ye were sealed with that holy Spirit of promise,**</u>
>
> 14 **Which [Who] is the earnest of our inheritance until the redemption of the purchased possession, unto the praise of his glory.**

At the moment of salvation, the transaction is initiated. The believer is immediately saved and receives the Holy Spirit Who is called the "earnest" of our inheritance. This "earnest" is the deposit that secures the completion of the transaction which occurs at the Rapture. Ephesians 1:13-14:

> 13 **In whom ye also trusted, after that ye heard the word of truth, <u>the gospel of your salvation</u>: in whom also after that ye believed, <u>ye were sealed with that holy Spirit of promise</u>, 14 <u>Which is the</u>**

earnest of our inheritance until the re-
demption of the purchased possession,
unto the praise of his glory.

Grace Believers are bought with Christ's blood. We are His purchased possession and spiritually placed *in Christ* Who is seated beside the Father. We remain here on earth in our bodies, yet we are assured of the full completion of our redemption! How? We have the holy Spirit of Promise Who guarantees it. The fulfillment of our bodily redemption occurs at the Rapture. Friend, there is wonderful news for those saved by grace through faith. We have an inheritance in Christ which far exceeds our salvation! The book *Ephesians: Dispensationally Considered* provides a detailed explanation.

Paul remained in Ephesus to teaches both Jews and Gentiles for three months. Acts 19:8:

8 And he went into the synagogue, and spake boldly for the space of three months, disputing and persuading the things concerning the kingdom of God.

Many there believed. In response to this, a wave of opposition came against him. Having already reached those who would believe, he left the synagogue, but continued teaching all who would listen for two years. Verses 9-10:

> 9 But when divers [many] were hardened, and believed not, but spake evil of that way before the multitude, he [Paul] departed from them, and separated the disciples, disputing daily in the school of one Tyrannus.

> 10 And this continued by the space of two years; so that all they which dwelt in Asia heard the word of the Lord Jesus, both Jews and Greeks.

The Apostle Paul is not known for performing miracles, signs, and wonders. These were promised to the Jews by God as a means of validating His prophets. He did perform some during his earlier ministry. Verses 11-12:

> 11 And God wrought [worked] special miracles by the hands of Paul: 12 So that from his body were brought unto the sick handkerchiefs or aprons, and the diseases departed from them, and the evil spirits went out of them.

It was God's way of making people aware of Paul's

ministry. As a result, many came to hear what Paul had to say.

As Paul became more widely known, there was a sorcerer who attempted to do miracles in Paul's name. Verses 13-17:

> 13 Then certain of the vagabond Jews, exorcists, took upon them to call [pronounce] over them which had evil spirits the name of the Lord Jesus, saying, We adjure you by Jesus whom Paul preacheth. 14 And there were seven sons of one Sceva, a Jew, and chief of the priests, which did so.

> 15 And the evil spirit answered and said, Jesus I know, and Paul I know; but who are ye? 16 And the man in whom the evil spirit was [he] leaped on them, and overcame them, and prevailed against them, so that they fled out of that house naked and wounded.

> 17 And this was known to all the Jews and Greeks [Gentiles] also dwelling at Ephesus; and fear fell on them all, and the name of the Lord Jesus was magnified.

This began a period of great evangelism for the Gospel of Grace. People now listened in fear. They turned away from their dark arts which caused the Word of God to spread far and wide. Verses 18-20:

> 18 **And many that believed came, and confessed, and shewed their deeds.**
>
> 19 **Many of them also which used curi-ous arts brought their books together, and burned them before all men: and they counted the price of them, and found it fifty thousand pieces of silver.**
>
> 20 **So mightily grew the word of God and prevailed.**

When the notoriety of these events died down, Paul made plans to travel from Ephesus to Macedonia north of Greece. Then, he planned to head to Achaia which was at the southern end of Greece. He had not forgotten his promise to the Apostles at Jerusalem. After he delivered the alms to Jerusalem, he planned to go to Rome. Verse 21:

> 21 **After these things were ended, Paul purposed in the spirit, when he had passed through Macedonia and Achaia,**

to go to Jerusalem, saying, After I have
been there, I must also see Rome.

Paul sent Timothy and Erastus ahead to Macedonia
while he tarried in present-day Turkey. Verse 22:

22 So he sent into Macedonia two of
them that ministered unto him, Timotheus and Erastus; but he himself
stayed in Asia for a season.

As Paul remained behind, the spiritual opposition saw an opportunity to attack him. Ephesus
was a prosperous seaport with many ships coming
and going. It was also a center of commerce with
one of the largest temples dedicated to the goddess
Diana. A large silver trade was supported by the
selling of silver charms and mementoes having al-
leged magical powers. This was "big business!"
Verses 23-26:

23 And the same time there arose no
small stir about that way. 24 For a certain man named Demetrius, a silver-
smith, which made silver shrines for
Diana, brought no small gain [profit]
unto the craftsmen;

25 Whom he called together with the

workmen of like occupation, and said, Sirs, ye know that by this craft we have our wealth.

26 Moreover ye see and hear, that not alone at Ephesus, but almost throughout all Asia, this Paul hath persuaded and turned away much people, saying that they be no gods, which are made with hands:

These merchants were concerned with their income and livelihood. It quickly became a matter of religious persecution by claiming Diana's "magnificence" was being destroyed. Verse 27:

27 So that not only this our craft is in danger to be set at nought [to nothing]; but also that the temple of the great goddess Diana should be despised, and her magnificence should be destroyed, whom all Asia and the world worshippeth.

A mob was incited and they were whipped into a frenzy. Two of Paul's companions and fellow workers in the gospel were grabbed as everyone rushed into the theater. Verses 28-29:

254

28 And when they heard these sayings, they were full of wrath, and cried out, saying, Great is Diana of the Ephesians.

29 And the whole city was filled with confusion: and having caught Gaius and Aristarchus, men of Macedonia, Paul's companions in travel, they rushed with one accord [mind] into the theatre.

During all of this commotion, Paul intended to enter the theater, but he was prevented by the other believers. This, no doubt, saved his life since God had more work for him to accomplish. Verses 30-31:

30 And when Paul would have entered in unto the people, the disciples suffered [allowed] him not.

31 And certain of the chief of Asia, which were his friends, sent unto him, desiring him that he would not adventure himself into the theatre.

Inside the theater, tension was high. Most of the crowd did not know why they were there. Verse 32:

32 Some therefore cried one thing, and some another: for the assembly was confused; and the more part knew not wherefore they were come together.

One of Paul's companions, Alexander, was put forward to speak. However, because he was a Jew, the crowd ignored him and the pandemonium continued. Verses 33-34:

33 And they drew Alexander out of the multitude, the Jews putting him forward. And Alexander beckoned with the hand, and would have made his defence unto the people. **34** But when they knew that he was a Jew, all with one voice about the space of two hours cried out, Great is Diana of the Ephesians.

Finally, someone with civil authority arrived and was able to silence the mob by addressing them. Verses 35-37:

35 And when the town clerk had appeased the people, he said, Ye men of Ephesus, what man is there that knoweth not how that the city of the Ephesians is a worshipper of the great goddess Diana, and of the image which fell down from Jupiter?

36 Seeing then that these things cannot be spoken against, ye ought to be quiet, and to do nothing rashly. 37 For ye have brought hither [here] these men, which are neither robbers of churches, nor yet blasphemers of your goddess.

The clerk tells them, if this is a legal matter, then there are courts who will hear the case. Verses 38-39:

38 Wherefore if Demetrius, and the craftsmen which are with him, have a matter against any man, the law is open, and there are deputies: let them implead [bring suit against] one another. 39 But if ye enquire anything concerning other matters, it shall be determined in a lawful assembly.

Whatever citizens do, it must be determined by a lawful assembly. The clerk warns them that this assembly is not lawful. They should disband immediately before the Roman authorities become aware. Should that happen, it would not go well for them. Verses 40-41:

40 For we are in danger to be called in question for this day's uproar, there being no cause whereby we may give an account of this concourse. **41** And when he had thus spoken, he dismissed the assembly.

NOTES:

When I teach, I like to offer personal comments that are not part of the class. Here, I feel there is an important point I would like you to take away from this chapter. It has to do with the many uses of the word "church." The word "church" could mean a building such as "Our church is brick." It could mean a service. "What time is 'church?'" It could also be used to refer to the universal believers. Unless someone explains their use of the word "church," it can be confusing. What does this have to do with Acts 19?

The word "church" comes from the Greek word ἐκκλησία or ekklesia which literally means "the called-out ones." It is to refer to a smaller group or "subset" taken out of a larger group. Here, in Acts 19, the Greek word ἐκκλησία appears three times. Here, the translators chose to use the word "assembly" each time. However, in this case, the "subset" is the unruly mob! Each time, the translators could have used "church," but instead used "assembly" because of the context.

Verse 32:

> 32 Some therefore cried one thing, and some another: for the <u>assembly</u> was confused; and the more part knew not wherefore [the reason] they were [had] come together.

Verse 39:

> 39 But if ye enquire anything concerning other matters, it shall be determined in a lawful <u>assembly</u>.

Verse 41:

> 41 And when he had thus spoken, he dismissed the <u>assembly</u>.

Yet, in the Greek text, Luke chose to use the word "ekklesia" which the translators rightfully chose the word "assembly" rather than "church." So, why am I making this such an important point?

During my earlier years in seminary, I was

reading one of my required textbooks. It referred to Israel as "the Church in the Wilderness." What? I thought the church started in the New Testament. So what was "the Church" doing in the Wilderness with Moses? Since Israel was "called out" from among all the other nations, the author of that text-book used the word "church." Yes, Israel is a sub-set. Yes, they were "called-out" from all the nations to be God's holy or separate people. Unfortunately, this became the basis of a huge misinterpretation of Scripture! Allow me to explain.

There are many who teach that "any" group of people who are "called out" by God are one and the same "church" regardless of who they are or when they were "called out." They have wrongly concluded and teach that God's one true "church" was Israel. They assume that God can only "call out" one group of people. That is like saying a man can only be the father of one child. Yes, Abraham's children are "the ones" to whom God promised the Kingdom. They are also "the ones" who must follow the Law of Moses and the Kingdom Gospel preached by their Messiah. They could be called the "Kingdom Church." However, there is another completely different subset of people who were "called-out" by God and they are *not* Israel.

God gave the Gospel of Grace to the Apostle Paul to bring to the Gentiles. This salvation message is open to any individual who chooses to believe – whether they be Jew or Gentile. For those who choose to accept God's gift by believing in the finished work of Christ, they too are the "called out" ones. Paul refers to them as the Body of Christ. He wrote, "Now ye are the body of Christ, and members in particular [individually]" (1 Cor. 12:27).

Personally, I avoid using the word "church" because of this confusion. Instead, I use the word "assembly." There are a great number of people who consider "the church" to be God's singularly chosen people regardless of the historical context. Yet, God has chosen to "call out" more than one group of people. In fact, there are two groups that He has "called out" for His purpose. They are the "Kingdom Believers" and the "Grace Believers." As we continue with our study of Acts, I am confident that you will clearly see the difference.

22

Acts 20

It was time for Paul to move on. He makes plans to go to Macedonia first and then to travel south into Greece. Acts 20:1-2:

> 1 **And after the uproar was ceased, Paul called unto him the disciples, and embraced them, and departed for to go into Macedonia.**
>
> 2 **And when he had gone over those parts, and had given them much exhortation, he came into Greece,**

While visiting the assemblies in Macedonia, he encouraged them. When he came to Greece, he would remain there for three months. Verse 3:

> 3 **And there [he] abode three months.**

And when the Jews laid wait for him, as he was about to sail into Syria, he purposed to return through Macedonia.

Before returning to Syria, the Jews forced him to change his plans. Instead of returning by ship, he would go by land and travel through Macedonia.

Luke tells us that on this trip, Paul would have seven traveling companions. Verse 4:

4 And there accompanied him into Asia Sopater of Berea; and of the Thessalonians, Aristarchus and Secundus; and Gaius of Derbe, and Timotheus; and of Asia, Tychicus and Trophimus.

Some went ahead and waited for him to arrive in Troas. He would come to them from Philippi after the Feast of Unleavened Bread. Verses 5-6:

5 These [companions] going before tarried for us at Troas. 6 And we sailed away from Philippi after the days of unleavened bread, and came unto them to Troas in five days; where we abode seven days.

During Creation, God rested on the seventh day. Jews still honor the seventh day, the Sabbath, in remembrance of His day of rest. Christians choose to gather on the first day of the week, Sunday, to remember His resurrection. Verse 7:

7 **And upon the first day of the week, when the disciples came together to break bread, Paul preached unto them, ready to depart on the morrow [next day]; and [he] continued his speech until midnight.**

On this particular day, Paul had taught well into the evening. People had gathered in a room on the third floor. Lit by many torches, the room was oppressively warm. A young man sat in the cool of the window. Verses 8-9:

8 **And there were many lights in the upper chamber, where they were gathered together.** 9 **And there sat in a window a certain young man named Eutychus, being fallen into a deep sleep: and as Paul was long preaching, he sunk down with sleep, and fell down from the third loft [floor], and was taken up dead.**

Paul went down to where the body lay lifeless on the ground below. Verses 10-12:

10 **And Paul went down, and fell on him, and embracing him said, Trouble not yourselves; for his life is in him.**

11 **When he therefore was come [brought] up again, and had broken bread, and eaten, and talked a long while, even till break of day, so he [Paul] departed.**

12 **And they brought the young man alive, and were not a little comforted.**

We can easily forget Luke is the writer. In the next verse, he includes himself saying that "we" sailed to meet Paul because he was determined to go by foot. Traveling by ship would have made the journey shorter and easier. However, by doing so, he had foiled the plans of the Jews. Verses 13-16:

13 **And we went before to [ahead by] ship, and sailed unto Assos, there intending to take in Paul: for so had he appointed, minding himself to go afoot.**

14 And when he met with us at Assos, we took him in [aboard], and came [sailed] to Mitylene.

15 And we sailed thence, and came the next day over against [near] Chios; and the next day we arrived at Samos, and tarried at Trogyllium; and the next day we came to Miletus.

16 For Paul had determined to sail by Ephesus, because he would not spend the time in Asia: for he hasted [hurried], if [so] it were possible for him, to be at Jerusalem [by] the day of Pentecost.

As you remember, Pentecost is the Festival of the First Fruits. This celebration of the harvest occurs fifty days after Passover.

Stopping at various ports along their course, Paul continued teaching and strengthening believers. He sent a message ahead to Ephesus and asked the elders to meet him upon his arrival there. The following recounts this meeting. Verses 17-18:

17 And from Miletus he sent to Ephesus, and called the elders of the church.

18 **And when they were come to him, he said unto them, Ye know, from the first day that I came into Asia, after what manner I have been with you at all seasons,**

He reminds them of the time they spent together and how he served them as their Apostle. Verses 19-21:

19 **Serving the Lord with all humility of mind, and with many tears, and temptations, which befell me by the lying in wait of the Jews:**

20 **And how I kept back [withheld] nothing that was profitable unto you, but have shewed you, and have taught you publicly, and from house to house,**

21 **Testifying both to the Jews, and also to the Greeks, repentance toward God, and faith toward our Lord Jesus Christ.**

Paul remained in God's will. Regardless of the cost, his course was fixed and he was determined to follow it. We can sense the finality of this meeting. Verses 22-24:

268

22 And now, behold, I go bound in the spirit unto Jerusalem, not knowing the things that shall befall me there: **23** Save [Except] that the Holy Ghost witnesseth in every city, saying that bonds and afflictions abide me.

24 But none of these things move me, neither count I my life dear unto myself, so that I might finish my course with joy, and the ministry, which I have received of [from] the Lord Jesus, to testify the gospel of the grace of God.

This would be the last time they would see him face to face. Sorrow filled their hearts. Verses 25-27:

25 And now, behold, I know that ye all, among whom I have gone preaching the kingdom of God, shall see my face no more. **26** Wherefore I take you to record [remember] this day, that I am pure from the blood of all men. **27** For I have not shunned [avoided] to declare unto you all the counsel of God.

As Moses had warned the Jews before his death,

Paul also warns them of what will happen once he is gone. He speaks about "grievous wolves" who will come to feast on those who are not careful. Think of the present-day churches. They will pollute the simplicity of the Gospel of Grace and corrupt what Paul had taught them. Even ministers from within will rise up and be self-serving; not caring about true doctrine. Here, he speaks to the elders in verses 28-31:

> 28 **Take heed therefore unto yourselves, and to all the flock, over the which the Holy Ghost hath made you overseers, to feed the church of God, which he hath purchased with his own blood.**
>
> 29 **For I know this, that after my departing shall grievous wolves enter in among you, not sparing the flock.** 30 **Also of your own selves shall men arise, speaking perverse things, to draw away disciples after them.**
>
> 31 **Therefore watch, and remember, that by the space of three years I ceased not to warn every one night and day with tears.**

The time was short for Paul to reach Jerusalem by

Pentecost. So, he bid them farewell with a blessing and prayer. Verse 32:

> 32 **And now, brethren, I commend you to God, and to the word of his grace, which is able to build you up, and to give you an inheritance among all them which are sanctified.**

He reminds them of his selfless service to them. While he was with them, he supported both his own needs as well as those who were with him by the work of his own hands. Verses 33-35:

> 33 **I have coveted no man's silver, or gold, or apparel. 34 Yea, ye yourselves know, that these hands have minis-tered unto my necessities, and to them that were with me.**

> 35 **I have shewed you all things, how that so labouring ye ought to support the weak, and to remember the words of the Lord Jesus, how he said, It is more blessed to give than to receive.**

As they parted, they were overwhelmed with sorrow. They knew they would not see their be-loved apostle and friend again. They walked with him to the ship and bid him farewell. Verses 36-38:

> 36 **And when he had thus spoken, he kneeled down, and prayed with them all. 37 And they all wept sore, and fell on Paul's neck, and kissed him,**
>
> 38 **Sorrowing most of all for the words which he spake, that they should see his face no more. And they accompanied him unto the ship.**

Imagine this group of believers from the assembly in Ephesus standing on the shore waving until the ship was out of sight. As they turned and headed to their homes, they thought about Paul's words. As he sat upon the ship, he worried about what would become of them.

23

Acts 21

From Ephesus, they sailed east and stopped briefly at several ports along the Mediterranean Sea. At that time, many people booked passage on cargo ships. In this case, their ship stopped at the following ports of call: Coos, Rhodes, and Patara. Changing ships, they continued eastward. Sailing below Cyprus, they came to Tyre. Acts 21:1-3:

> 1 And it came to pass, that after we were gotten from them [in Ephesus], and had launched, we came with a straight course unto Coos, and the day following unto Rhodes, and from thence unto Patara:
>
> 2 And finding a ship sailing over unto Phenicia, we went aboard, and set forth. 3 Now when we had discovered

Cyprus, we left [kept] it on the [our] left hand, and sailed into Syria, and landed at Tyre: for there the ship was to unlade her burden [unload cargo].

The believers in Tyre warned him not to continue to Jerusalem. However, Paul's mind was set and he could not be dissuaded. Verse 4:

4 And finding disciples, we tarried there seven days: who said to Paul through the Spirit, that he should not go up to Jerusalem.

Like with the believers in Ephesus, Paul had a close bond with his hosts. When their visit ended, they also walked with him to the ship and parted with prayer. Verses 5-6:

5 And when we had accomplished those days, we departed and went our way; and they all brought us on our way, with wives and children, till we were out of the city: and we kneeled down on the shore, and prayed.

6 And when we had taken our leave one of another, we took ship; and they returned home again.

Once on a ship again, they cleared the port of Tyre and headed south along the most eastern shore of the Mediterranean Sea. Ptolemais was south of Tyre. From Ptolemais, they navigated their way to Caesarea. This was the port nearest to Jerusalem. Verses 7-8:

7 And when we had finished our course from Tyre, we came to Ptolemais, and saluted the brethren, and abode with them one day.

8 And the next day we that were of Paul's company departed, and came unto Caesarea: and we entered into the house of Philip the evangelist, which was one of the seven; and abode with him.

Philip, along with Stephen, were of the seven chosen by the Apostles in Jerusalem to care for the Kingdom Believers. (See Acts 6:5.) Philip was an evangelist and preached the Gospel of the Kingdom. Directed by the Holy Spirit, he explained the Scriptures to the eunuch, a Gentile, whom he later baptized. (See Acts 8:1-40.)

While they stayed with Philip, Paul was again warned not to go to Jerusalem. Verses 9-12:

9 And the same man had four daughters, virgins, which did prophesy. 10 And as we tarried there many days, there came down from Judaea a certain prophet, named Agabus.

11 And when he was come unto us, he took Paul's girdle, and bound his own hands and feet, and said, Thus saith the Holy Ghost, So shall the Jews at Jerusalem bind the man that owneth this girdle, and shall deliver him into the hands of the Gentiles.

12 And when we heard these things, both we, and they of that place, besought him not to go up to Jerusalem.

The Lord made Paul aware of this from the beginning of his ministry. Do you remember the Lord's response to Ananias? He told him, "For I will shew him how great things he must suffer for my name's sake" (Acts 9:16). The Lord had assured him He would be with him. So, Paul remained resolved to hold true to his course. Verses 13-14:

13 Then Paul answered, What mean ye to [Why do you] weep and to break mine heart? for I am ready not to be

bound only, but also to die at Jerusalem for the name of the Lord Jesus.

14 And when he would not be persuaded, we ceased, [by] saying, The will of the Lord be done.

They stayed with Philip for a while and, when they departed, several believers accompanied them. One man owned a house where they could stay in Jerusalem. Verses 15-17:

15 And after those days we took up our carriages, and went up to Jerusalem. 16 There went with us also certain of the disciples of Caesarea, and brought with them one Mnason of Cyprus, an old disciple, with whom we should lodge.

17 And when we were come to [arrived at] Jerusalem, the brethren received us gladly.

Arriving safely in Jerusalem, they were warmly greeted by the believers there.

Not wanting to delay, Paul went the next day to see the other Apostles. He desired to make a report to them concerning the Gospel of Grace. There was also the matter of the alms he had collected. Verses 18-19:

> 18 **And the day following Paul went in with us unto James; and all the elders were present.**

> 19 **And when he had saluted them, he declared particularly what things God had wrought [accomplished] among the Gentiles by his ministry.**

Likewise, the Twelve reported how God had prospered them with the Gospel of the Kingdom. Verse 20:

> 20 **And when they heard it, they glorified the Lord, and said unto him, Thou seest, brother, how many thousands of Jews there are which believe; and they are all zealous of the law:**

Notice these last words: "they are all zealous of the Law." This is the "distinguishing factor" between the two gospels. They gave Paul letters concerning the application of the Law to new Gentile believers. As they continue, do you perceive a change in their tone? Verses 21-22:

278

21 **And they are informed [aware] of thee, <u>that thou teachest all the Jews which are among the Gentiles</u> to forsake Moses, saying that they ought not to circumcise their children, neither to walk after the customs.**

22 **What is it therefore? the multitude must needs come together: for they will hear that thou art come.**

This is not about Gentiles being required to follow the Law. It is about the Jews who accept the Gospel of Grace. Paul teaches that all Grace Believers are no longer "under" the Law, but are "under" grace. This applies to "all" who are saved by grace through faith. Paul explains this in Romans 6:14:

14 **For sin shall not have dominion over you: <u>for ye are not under the law, but under grace.</u>**

Apparently, the Jewish Apostles did not understand this. They tell Paul he needs to explain himself to the Jewish believers.

These Apostles recommend that he follow the Jewish customs and traditions before he meets with the local Jews. Acts 12:23-24:

23 Do therefore this that we say to thee: We have four men which have a vow on them;

24 Them take, and purify thyself with them, and be at charges with them, that they may shave their heads: <u>and all may know that those things, whereof they were informed concerning thee, are nothing; but that thou thyself also walkest orderly, and keepest the law.</u>

What Paul teaches the Jews saved by the Gospel of Grace is in conflict with what the Twelve teach under the Gospel of the Kingdom. Therefore, they suggest Paul make a visible showing to all the Jews that he "walkest orderly, and keepest the Law" (v. 24).

The Apostles hold that Paul, being a Jew, must still observe the Law. However, the Gentiles are absolved from the requirements of the Law, but with some exceptions. Verse 25:

25 As touching the Gentiles which believe, we have written and concluded that they observe no such thing, save only that they keep themselves from things offered to idols, and from blood

and from strangled, and from fornication.

The following has similarities to the events leading up to the Lord's crucifixion. Verses 26-27:

> 26 Then Paul took the men, and the next day purifying himself with them entered into the temple, to signify the accomplishment of the days of purification, until that an offering should be offered for every one of them.

> 27 And when the seven days were almost ended, the Jews which were of Asia, when they saw him in the temple, stirred up all the people, and laid hands on him,

From this point, there will be no turning back. The Jews in Jerusalem were unfamiliar with Paul. However, the Jews from Asia Minor were familiar both him and his gospel. They are the ones who created the commotion and chaos ensued. Verses 28-30:

> 28 Crying out, Men of Israel, help: This is the man, that teacheth all men everywhere against the people [Jews], and the law, and this place: and further

brought Greeks also into the temple, and hath polluted this holy place.

29 (For they had seen before with him in the city Trophimus an Ephesian, whom they [falsely] supposed that Paul had brought into the temple.)

30 And all the city was moved, and the people ran together: and they took Paul, and drew him out of the temple: and forthwith the doors were shut.

Such a dramatic show! They closed the huge temple doors as if they were under siege. As you can image, panic and chaos ensued.

The Jews from Asia Minor had doggedly pursued Paul. They are the same ones who persecuted him throughout his mission. There was a religious, almost self-righteous, hatred towards Paul and his teachings. Truth is often ignored or, in this case, violently rejected. Here, they sought to kill Paul! With such an uproar, it brought an immediate response from the Roman authorities charged with keeping peace in this volatile country. Verses 31-33:

31 And as they went about to kill him, tidings came unto the chief captain of

the band, that all Jerusalem was in an uproar. 32 Who immediately took soldiers and centurions, and ran down unto them: and when they saw the chief captain and the soldiers, they left [stopped their] beating of Paul.

33 Then the chief captain came near, and took him, and commanded him to be bound with two chains; and demanded who he was, and what he had done.

In the confusion, there were a variety of conflicting accusations made against Paul. The captain decided to bring him into the castle. Verses 34-36:

34 And some cried one thing, some another, among the multitude: and when he could not know the certainty for the tumult, he commanded him to be carried into the castle.

35 And when he came upon the stairs, so it was, that he was borne of [carried by] the soldiers for [because of] the violence of the people. 36 For the multitude of the people followed after, crying, Away with him.

As he was being escorted to the castle for safety, we can picture it. He was being ushered by the soldiers through the crowd as they attempted to lay hold of him.

As he was about to enter the castle, Paul turns to the soldiers and asks if he could address the crowd. The Romans had no idea who he was and believed him to be a criminal. Verses 37-38:

> 37 **And as Paul was to be led into the castle, he said unto the chief captain, May I speak unto thee? Who said, Canst thou speak Greek?**

> 38 **Art not thou that Egyptian, which before these days madest an uproar, and leddest out into the wilderness four thousand men that were murderers?**

In his response, Paul explains who he is and asks that he be allowed to speak to the people. Verse 39:

> 39 **But Paul said, I am a man which am a Jew of Tarsus, a city in Cilicia, a citizen of no mean city: and, I beseech thee, suffer [allow] me to speak unto the people.**

Having been granted permission to speak, he motioned to the angry crowd of Jews and they become silent. Verse 40:

> 40 **And when he had given him licence [permission], Paul stood on the stairs, and beckoned with the hand unto the people. And when there was made a great silence, he spake unto them in the Hebrew tongue, saying,**

We are blessed because Luke recorded the contents of Paul's speech for us in Acts 22.

24

Acts 22

Just for a moment, let our imagination set the scene. The Roman garrison was stationed in a castle not far from the Temple. Volatility in the region, especially in Jerusalem, was common. Thus, they were prepared to respond quickly. They were able to protect Paul from the mob until they ascertained the cause. The alarm was heard and the crowd grew to find out its cause. A great mass of people had now gathered and stood before him. The Romans granted Paul permission to speak.

He begins to address a crowd comprised almost exclusively of Jews by calling them "brethren and fathers." Acts 22:1-3:

> 1 **Men, brethren, and fathers, hear ye my defence which I make now unto you.** 2 **(And when they heard that he**

spake in the Hebrew tongue to them, they kept the more silence: and he saith,)

3 I am verily [truly] a man which am a Jew, born in Tarsus, a city in Cilicia, yet brought up in this city at the feet of Gamaliel, and taught according to the perfect manner of the law of the fathers, and was zealous toward God, as ye all are this day.

Although it was some time ago, he reminds them that he was the one who persecuted the followers of Jesus Christ called "the way." Few in the crowd were not followers of Christ because most of the Kingdom Believers had left Jerusalem due to persecution. This crowd was the pious Jews who were committed to the Mosaic Law, as well as the customs and traditions of their religion. Verses 4-5:

4 And I persecuted this [those of the] way unto the death, binding and delivering [them] into prisons both men and women.

5 As also the high priest doth bear me witness, and all the estate of the elders: from whom also I received letters unto

the brethren, and [I] went to Damascus,
to bring them which were there bound
unto Jerusalem, for to be punished.

He wanted to establish a connection with the audience. He was, like them, a zealous Jew.

He shares with them his personal encounter
with the Lord. The Jews understood divine inter-
vention. In fact, Paul's details are very similar to
those surrounding God's face-to-face meeting with
Moses. Verses 6-9:

> 6 And it came to pass, that, as I made
> my journey, and was come nigh unto
> [near to] Damascus about noon, sud-
> denly there shone from heaven a great
> light round about me. 7 And I fell unto
> the ground, and heard a voice saying
> unto me, Saul, Saul, why persecutest
> thou me?
>
> 8 And I answered, Who art thou, Lord?
> And he said unto me, I am Jesus of
> Nazareth, whom thou persecutest. 9
> And they that were with me saw in-
> deed the light, and were afraid; but
> they heard not the voice of him that
> spake to me.

God had spoken to Moses from the burning bush and, likewise, God gave instructions to Paul as to what he should do. The crowd listened. Verses 10-11:

> 10 And I said, What shall I do, Lord? And the Lord said unto me, Arise, and go into Damascus; and there it shall be told thee of all things which are appointed for thee to do.

> 11 And when I could not see for the glory of that light, being led by the hand of [by] them that were with me, I came into Damascus.

Previously, we looked at these verses. We used them to establish the validity of Paul's mission according to God's response to Ananias. Here, Paul shares this with the crowd. Verses 12-16:

> 12 And one Ananias, a devout man according to the law, having a good report of all the Jews which dwelt there,

> 13 Came unto me, and stood, and said unto me, Brother Saul, receive thy sight. And the same hour I looked up upon him.

14 And he said, The God of our fathers hath chosen thee, that thou shouldest know his will, and see that Just One [the Messiah], and shouldest hear the voice of his mouth.

15 For thou shalt be his witness unto all men of what thou hast seen and heard. **16** And now why tarriest thou? arise, and be baptized, and wash away thy sins, calling on the name of the Lord.

God had warned Paul that those in Jerusalem will not accept his testimony and he should leave there. Verses 17-18:

17 And it came to pass, that, when I was come again to Jerusalem, even while I prayed in the temple, I was in a trance;

18 And saw him saying unto me, Make haste, and get thee quickly out of Jerusalem: for they will not receive thy testimony concerning me.

Paul disagrees. He tells the Lord these people know him and his fight against those who followed "the way." Verses 19-20:

19 **And I said, Lord, they know that I imprisoned and beat in every synagogue them that believed on thee:** 20 **And when the blood of thy martyr Stephen was shed, I also was standing by, and consenting unto his death, and kept [watched over] the raiment of them that slew him.**

God replied to Paul with a command. Verse 21:

21 **And he said unto me, <u>Depart: for I will send thee far hence unto the Gentiles</u>.**

When he mentioned God sending him to "the Gentiles," he loses his audience. Verses 22-23:

22 **And they gave him audience unto [up until] this word, and then lifted up their voices, and said, Away with such a fellow from the earth: for it is not fit that he should live.** 23 **And as they cried out, and cast off their clothes, and threw dust into the air,**

Once again, they became the angry mob. The captain of the Roman guard ordered that Paul be brought inside for his safety. Verse 24:

24 The chief captain commanded him to be brought into the castle, and bade [ordered] that he should be examined by scourging; that he [the captain] might know wherefore [why] they cried so against him.

The Romans used a physical form of interrogation. They would basically beat the truth out of someone. Paul informs the centurion that he was a Roman citizen. As you will see, this put everything in a different light. Verses 25-29:

25 And as they bound him with thongs, Paul said unto the centurion that stood by, Is it lawful for you to scourge a man that is a Roman, and uncondemned? **26** When the centurion heard that, he went and told the chief captain, saying, Take heed what thou doest: for this man is a Roman.

27 Then the chief captain came, and said unto him, Tell me, art thou a Roman? He said, Yea. **28** And the chief captain answered, With a great sum obtained I this freedom. And Paul said, But I was free born.

29 Then straightway [immediately] they departed from him which should have examined him: and the chief captain also was afraid, after he knew that he [Paul] was a Roman, and because he had bound him [Paul].

We will see the importance of Paul's Roman citizenship and how it will affect his future.

The next day, they summoned the chief priests and the council to appear. This is the same council that had Stephen put to death. The Romans needed to know what were their charges against Paul. Verse 30:

30 On the morrow, because he [the captain] would have known the certainty wherefore [wanted to know with certainty why] he was accused of the Jews, he loosed him from his bands, and commanded the chief priests and all their council to appear, and brought Paul down, and set him before them.

Paul stood face to face with his accusers. They must now present their charges against him.

25

Acts 23

Brought before his accusers, Paul looks at them intently before making his speech. Acts 23:1-2:

> **1 And Paul, earnestly beholding the council, said, Men and brethren, I have lived in all good conscience before God until this day.**
>
> **2 And the high priest Ananias commanded them that stood by him to smite [strike] him on the mouth.**

Notice Paul's response in verse 3:

> **3 Then said Paul unto him, God shall smite thee, thou whited [whitewashed] wall: for sittest thou to judge me after the law, and commandest me**

to be smitten contrary to the law?

Those who accuse him of breaking the Mosaic Law have themselves now broken the Law by striking him. Trained as a Pharisee, he was as knowledgeable of the Law as they were.

Their hatred of Paul from these self-righteous Jews was palpable. Verses 4-5:

> **4 And they that stood by said, Revilest thou God's high priest? 5 Then said Paul, I wist [knew] not, brethren, that he was the high priest: for it is written, Thou shalt not speak evil of the ruler of thy people.**

Perhaps they were all dressed similarly and Paul was not aware of the High Priest's presence. He realizes both Sadducees and Pharisees present. These two groups are notably divided concerning the resurrection. The former denying it, while the latter does not. Verse 6:

> **6 But when Paul perceived that the one part were Sadducees, and the other Pharisees, he cried out in the council, Men and brethren, I am a Pharisee, the son of a Pharisee: <u>of the hope and res-</u>**

urrection of the dead I am called in question.

Now, watch the sparks fly between these two opposing groups. Their hatred for each other could not be contained. Verses 7-9:

> 7 **And when he had so said, there arose a dissension [argument] between the Pharisees and the Sadducees: and the multitude was divided. 8 For the Sadducees say that there is no resurrection, neither angel, nor spirit: but the Pharisees confess both.**
>
> 9 **And there arose a great cry: and the scribes that were of the Pharisees' part arose, and strove, saying, We find no evil in this man: but if a spirit or an angel hath spoken to him, let us not fight against God.**

The Roman captain, who was unbiased, could see these men who were bringing charges against Paul could not agree among themselves. Those of the Pharisees who believe in the resurrection from the dead said, "We find no evil in this man" (v. 9). In the midst of this ruckus, Paul was being yanked back and forth. So, the chief captain removed him and returned him to the castle. Verse 10:

> 10 **And when there arose a great dissension, the chief captain, fearing lest Paul should have been pulled in pieces of them, commanded the soldiers to go down, and to take him by force from among them, and to bring him into the castle.**

The next night, while Paul was being held in protective custody inside the castle, the Lord spoke to him. Verse 11:

> 11 **And the night following the Lord stood by him, and said, Be of good cheer, Paul: for as thou hast testified of me in Jerusalem, so must thou bear witness also at Rome.**

God had told Ananias, "Go thy way: for he is a chosen vessel unto me, to bear my name before the Gentiles, and kings, and the children of Israel" (Acts 9:15). The speech Paul made within the shadow of the Temple was to "the children of Israel." Now, he will appear before Caesar.

This evil and hatred could only come from Satan. Notice what Jesus said concerning these rulers in John 8:44:

> **44 Ye are of your father the devil, and the lusts of your father ye will do. <u>He was a murderer from the beginning, and abode not in the truth, because there is no truth in him</u>. When he speaketh a lie, he speaketh of his own: for he is a liar, and the father of it.**

Consider the depth of their hatred. Acts 23: 12-14:

> **12 And when it was day, certain of the Jews banded together, and bound themselves under a curse [oath], saying that they would neither eat nor drink till they had killed Paul. 13 And they were more than forty which had made this conspiracy.**
>
> **14 And they came to the chief priests and elders, and said, We have bound ourselves under a great curse, that we will eat nothing until we have slain Paul.**

This "curse" was the oath with the consequence of death should they fail. They planned to carry out premeditated murder and, if they did not succeed, then they pledged to die by starvation.

These forty conspired with the rulers of Israel to have Paul brought before them for additional questioning. This would provide them with the perfect opportunity to kill Paul. This sounds like a best-selling thriller! These evil men were plotting to murder the Apostle Paul with the foreknowledge of the priests and rulers of Israel. Verse 15:

> 15 **Now therefore ye with the council signify [suggest] to the chief captain that he bring him [Paul] down unto you tomorrow, as though ye would enquire something more perfectly concerning him: and we, or [when] ever he come near, are ready to kill him.**

Through divine providence, Paul's nephew was standing nearby and overheard their conversation! Verses 16-17:

> 16 **And when Paul's sister's son heard of their lying in wait, he went and entered into the castle, and told Paul.**
>
> 17 **Then Paul called one of the centurions unto him, and said, Bring this young man unto the chief captain: for**

he hath a certain thing to tell him.

The young man was presented to the chief captain. Verses 18-22:

18 So he took him, and brought him to the chief captain, and said, Paul the prisoner called me unto him, and prayed [asked] me to bring this young man unto thee, who hath something to say unto thee. 19 Then the chief captain took him by the hand, and went with him aside privately, and asked him, What is that thou hast to tell me?

20 And he said, The Jews have agreed to desire thee that thou wouldest bring down Paul tomorrow into the council, as though they would enquire somewhat of him more perfectly.

21 But do not thou yield unto them: for there lie in wait for him of them more than forty men, which have bound themselves with an oath, that they will neither eat nor drink till they have killed him: and now are they ready, looking for a promise from thee.

22 So the chief captain then let the young man depart, and charged him, See thou tell no man that thou hast shewed these things to me.

Upon learning of this plot to kill Paul, the chief captain reacts. As a result of this, look at the protection Paul receives. Unbeknownst to the Jews, he is taken from Jerusalem in safety! Verses 24-24:

23 And he called unto him two centurions, saying, Make ready two hundred soldiers to go to Caesarea, and horsemen threescore and ten [seventy] , and spearmen two hundred, at the third hour of the night;

24 And provide them beasts, that they may set Paul on, and bring him safe unto Felix the governor.

The Jewish custom is that night starts at 6 PM. So, their departure was about 9 PM.

The chief captain, named Claudius Lysias, wrote a letter to the governor which would accompany the prisoner. Verses 25-30:

25 And he wrote a letter after this man-

302

ner: 26 Claudius Lysias unto the most excellent governor Felix [I] sendeth greeting. 27 This man was taken of the Jews, and should have been killed of [by] them: then came I with an army, and rescued him, having understood that he was a Roman.

28 And when I would have known [wanted to know] the cause wherefore they accused him, I brought him forth into their council: 29 Whom I perceived to be accused of questions of their law, but to have nothing laid to his charge worthy of death or of bonds [imprisonment].

30 And when it was told me how that the Jews laid wait for the man, I sent [him] straightway to thee, and gave commandment to [told] his accusers also to say [speak] before thee what they had against him. Farewell.

Under cover of night, Paul was taken safely from the castle. The Jews who vowed to kill him knew nothing about this.

The soldiers followed orders and, brought

Paul safely to Antipatris. This was a city built in the first century BC by Herod the Great. It was about halfway between Jerusalem and Caesarea which was their destination. Verses 31-32:

> 31 **Then the soldiers, as it was com-manded them, took Paul, and brought him by night to Antipatris. 32 On the morrow they left the horsemen to go with him, and returned to the castle:**

Now safe in Antipatris, Paul had escaped the treachery with his location presently unknown. The horsemen returned to Jerusalem. Paul was not a prisoner because he was never convicted of a crime. He was held in protective custody until a proper interrogation could be made. Verse 33:

> 33 **Who, when they came to Caesarea, and [they] delivered the epistle [letter] to the governor, [and] presented Paul also before him.**

Upon reading the letter and hearing where Paul was found, the governor decides to hear the matter. Paul's accusers were summoned to appear. Paul remained in Roman protection. Verses 34-35:

> 34 **And when the governor had read the**

letter, he asked of what province he was. And when he understood that he was of Cilicia;

35 I will hear thee, said he, when thine accusers are also come. And he commanded him to be kept in Herod's judgment hall.

Paul would be held until his accusers could appear and, then, the governor would hear his case.

26

Acts 24

Jerusalem is located on a higher elevation. So, many biblical references speak about "going up to Jerusalem" or "coming down from Jerusalem." Such is the case here. Within the week, the High Priest and the elders arrived. This time, one person was chosen to speak on their behalf. Acts 24:1:

1 And after five days Ananias the high priest descended with the elders, and with a certain orator named Tertullus, who informed the governor against Paul.

When the hearing begins, Tertullus is called forward to present the charges against Paul. He begins by complimenting Felix who presided over the hearing. Verses 2-4:

2 And when he was called forth, Tertullus began to accuse him, saying, Seeing that by thee we enjoy great quietness, and that very worthy deeds are done unto this nation by thy providence, 3 We accept it always, and in all places, most noble Felix, with all thankfulness.

4 Notwithstanding, that I be not further tedious unto thee, I pray thee that thou wouldest hear us of thy clemency a few words.

Tertullus now presents his argument against Paul. Verses 5-9:

5 For we have found this man a pestilent fellow, and a mover of sedition among all the Jews throughout the world, and a ringleader of the sect of the Nazarenes:

6 Who also hath gone about to profane the temple: whom we took, and would have judged according to our law. 7 But the chief captain Lysias came upon us, and with great violence took him away out of our hands,

8 Commanding his accusers to come unto thee: by examining of whom thyself mayest take knowledge of all these things, whereof we accuse him.

9 And the Jews also assented, saying that these things were so.

This time, to everything Tertullus said, the Jews were all in agreement.

If we look at the actual charges, they appear to be pretty weak. Here are the charges for which Paul is accused. They found him to be: (1) a pestilent fellow, (2) a mover of sedition, (3) a ringleader of the sect of the Nazarenes, and (4) a profaner of the temple. If the Romans had not interfered, then Paul "would have [been] judged according to our law." When they said "our law" they refer to the Mosaic Law. In his response, Paul clearly states the true problem they have with him. Verse 10:

10 Then Paul, after that the governor had beckoned unto him to speak, answered, Forasmuch as I know that thou hast been of many years a judge unto this nation, I do the more cheerfully answer for myself:

It was less than two weeks since this all started, but the hatred of the Jewish leaders goes far deeper than that one incident. Verses 11-12:

> 11 **Because that thou mayest under-stand, that there are yet but twelve days since I went up to Jerusalem for to worship.**

> 12 **And they neither found me in the temple disputing with any man, neither raising up the people, neither in the synagogues, nor in the city:**

Those who followed after Christ were referred to as "the way." You will see that in Paul's speech below. Verses 13-15:

> 13 **Neither can they prove the things whereof they now accuse me. 14 But this I confess unto thee, that after <u>the way</u> which they call heresy, so worship I the God of my fathers, believing all things which are written in the law and in the prophets: 15 And have hope toward God, which they themselves also allow, that there shall be a resurrection of the dead, both of the just and unjust.**

Paul is not aware of anything he has done to offend either God or men. Verse 16:

16 And herein do I exercise myself, to have always a conscience void of offence toward God, and toward men.

Alms are specific donations or gifts intended for the poor and needy. The word "alms" comes from the Greek word meaning "pity or mercy." It had been a long time since Paul was in Jerusalem, but he came to bring relief to those who are suffering there. Verse 17:

17 Now after many years I came to bring alms to my nation, and offerings.

When Paul was in the Temple, he was alone. The Jews from Asia falsely accused him of bringing a Gentile into the temple. This was the basis for the charge of profaning the Temple. All of their charges were nothing more than hearsay and rumors from the Jews in Asia. Verses 18-20:

18 Whereupon certain Jews from Asia found me [being] purified in the temple, neither with [any] multitude, nor with [any] tumult.

19 Who ought to have been here before thee, and object, if they had ought [anything] against me.

20 Or else let these same [who are] here say, if they have found any evil doing in me, while I stood before the council,

Paul says these Jews from Asia are the ones who should be here accusing him. He previously stood before the Chief Priest and elders in Jerusalem and no charges were determined before Claudius Lysias, the chief captain. Now, they have appeared again. If they have anything against him, then let them say it now.

Paul cuts to the heart of the matter. Verse 21:

21 Except it be for this one voice [statement], that I cried standing among them, <u>Touching the resurrection of the dead I am called in question by you this day</u>.

This is the same matter that infuriated the Jews before. It is the very heart of Paul's Gospel of Grace! Not only that, if resurrection from the dead is not dependent upon works or religion, as Paul preached, then what value has their religion? This is a major affront to their religion. When Paul first arrived in Jerusalem, he was warned by the other Apostles. Acts 21:21-22:

21 And they [the Jews] are informed [aware] of thee, that thou teachest all the Jews which are among the Gentiles to forsake Moses, saying that they ought not to circumcise their children, neither to walk after the customs.

22 What is it therefore? the multitude must needs come together: for they will hear that thou art come.

Anyone who is saved by the Gospel of Grace, Jew or Gentile, is no longer under the Law but under grace. Paul was sharing this with the Jewish believers. This is what offended the religious leaders! This is the reason they were prosecuting him!

Initially, followers of the Gospel of the Kingdom were called followers of "the way." When Felix heard Paul's statements, he stopped the hearing. He decided to hear testimony from Claudius Lysias, the chief captain, who was familiar with the situation. Felix believed that his testimony should clear this matter up. Acts 24:22:

22 And when Felix heard these things, having more perfect knowledge of <u>that way</u>, he deferred them, and said, When Lysias the chief captain shall come down, I will know the uttermost of your matter.

Until that time, Paul would remain in protective custody with certain freedoms. This included allowing him visitors. Verse 23:

23 And he commanded a centurion to keep Paul, and to let him have liberty, and that he should forbid none of his acquaintance to minister or come unto him.

While they waited for Claudius Lysias to appear, Felix and wife sent for Paul privately. They were curious to hear more from him. Verses 24-25:

24 And after certain days, when Felix came with his wife Drusilla, which [who] was a Jewess, he sent for Paul, and heard him concerning the faith in Christ.

25 And as he reasoned of righteousness, temperance, and judgment to come,

Felix trembled, and answered, Go thy way for this time; when I have a convenient season [time], I will call for thee.

Being confronted with Paul's truth about judgment, Felix trembled. The burden of sin and guilt weighs heavily when judgment is mentioned!

Felix continued to call Paul before him. During their conversations, Paul always answered his questions truthfully. Beyond his curiosity, he was hoping for a bribe to release him. Verse 26:

26 He hoped also that money should have been given him of [by] Paul, that he might loose [release] him: wherefore he sent for him the oftener, and communed with him.

Paul remained incarcerated and this pleased the Jews. Verse 27:

27 But after two years Porcius Festus came into Felix' room: and Felix, willing to shew the Jews a pleasure, left Paul bound.

27

Acts 25

In the last hearing, Antonius Felix was the Roman procurator who heard Paul's case. Since then, he was replaced by Porcius Festus. This would be between 55 AD and 60 AD. Seeing that Festus had come to Jerusalem from Caesarea, the Jews seized the opportunity to influence this new procurator. They saw a chance to advance their designs against Paul. Here was their plan. Acts 25:1-3:

> 1 **Now when Festus was come into the province, after three days he ascended from Caesarea to Jerusalem.** 2 **Then the high priest and the chief of the Jews informed him against Paul, and besought him,** 3 **And desired favour against him [Paul], that he [Festus] would send for him to Jerusalem, laying wait in the way to kill him.**

Again, showing themselves to be righteous under the Law, they planned pre-meditated murder! Paul was a threat to them and their livelihood. As such, they determined he must die. Many times, the Jewish rulers would do the exact opposite of God's will. No wonder the Kingdom Gospel requires believers to prove their faith by works of righteousness until the Messiah returns!

Festus' response was impartial. He chose to leave Paul in Caesarea until his case could be heard. Verses 4-5:

> **4 But Festus answered, that Paul should be kept at Caesarea, and that he himself would depart shortly thither.**
>
> **5 Let them therefore, said he, which among you are able, go down with me, and accuse this man, if there be any wickedness in him.**

They would have ample opportunity to make their case against him. Being congenial, he invited them to accompany him on his return trip.

The distance between Jerusalem and Caesarea is about 120 kilometers or 75 miles. Verses 6-7:

6 And when he had tarried among them more than ten days, he went down unto Caesarea; and the next day sitting on the judgment seat commanded Paul to be brought.

7 And when he was come, the Jews which came down from Jerusalem stood round about, and laid many and grievous complaints against Paul, which they could not prove.

They made "many grievous complaints" against Paul, but none of them could be proven.

Paul offers his defense by stating that he has done nothing against either the laws of the Jews or the laws of Rome. Verses 8-11:

8 While he answered for himself, Neither against the law of the Jews, neither against the temple, nor yet against Caesar, have I offended anything at all.

9 But Festus, willing to do the Jews a pleasure, answered Paul, and said, Wilt thou go up to Jerusalem, and there be judged of these things before me?

10 Then said Paul, I stand at Caesar's judgment seat, where I ought to be judged: to the Jews have I done no wrong, as thou very well knowest.

11 For if I be an offender, or have committed anything worthy of death, I refuse not to die: but if there be none of these things whereof these accuse me, no man may deliver me unto them. <u>I appeal unto Caesar</u>.

This last line sealed the deal. As a Roman citizen, Paul had the right to appeal to Caesar which he did.

Notice Festus was far more faithful to the Roman law than these religious Jews were faithful to their Mosaic Law. Verse 12:

12 Then Festus, when he had conferred with the council, answered, Hast thou appealed unto Caesar? unto Caesar shalt thou go.

The Jewish accusers returned to Jerusalem. Paul remained safely in custody in Caesarea. King Agrippa and his queen came as royal guests of Festus. So, he shared with them these recent events. Verses 13-16:

13 And after certain days king Agrippa and Bernice came unto Caesarea to salute Festus.

14 And when they had been there many days, Festus declared Paul's cause unto the king, saying, There is a certain man left in bonds by Felix:

15 About whom, when I was at Jerusalem, the chief priests and the elders of the Jews informed me, desiring to have judgment against him.

16 To whom I answered, It is not the manner of the Romans to deliver any man to die, before that he which is accused have the accusers face to face, and have licence [permission] to answer for himself concerning the crime laid against him.

Festus continues to explain in verses 17-21:

17 Therefore, when they [his accusers] were come hither, without any delay on the morrow I sat on the judgment seat, and commanded the man to be brought forth.

18 Against whom when the accusers stood up, they brought none accusation of such things as I supposed: 19 But had certain questions against him of their own superstition, and of one Jesus, which was dead, whom Paul affirmed to be alive.

20 And because I doubted of such manner of questions, I asked him whether he would go to Jerusalem, and there be judged of these matters. 21 But when Paul had appealed to be reserved unto the hearing of Augustus, I commanded him to be kept till I might send him to Caesar.

All this made King Agrippa's curious and he told Festus he wished to hear Paul's matter. Do you remember God's words to Ananias saying that Paul would speak before kings? Verses 22-25:

22 Then Agrippa said unto Festus, I would also hear the man myself. To-morrow, said he, thou shalt hear him.

23 And on the morrow, when Agrippa was come, and Bernice, with great pomp, and was entered into the place

of hearing, with the chief captains, and principal men of the city, at Festus' commandment [orders] Paul was brought forth.

24 And Festus said, King Agrippa, and all men which are here present with us, ye see this man, about whom all the multitude of the Jews have dealt with me, both at Jerusalem, and also here, crying that he ought not to live any longer.

25 But when I found that he had committed nothing worthy of death, and that he himself hath appealed to [Caesar] Augustus, I have determined to send him.

Paul was exercising his right as a Roman citizen to appeal to Caesar. This also relieved Festus of any responsibility with regard to the Jews. He could figuratively throw up his hands. There was nothing else he could do. Besides appeasing King Agrippa's curiosity, there was another reason for Festus to convene this hearing. He could include King Agrippa's name on his letter when he sent Paul to Rome. Verses 26-27:

26 Of whom I have no certain thing to write unto my lord. Wherefore I have brought him forth before you, and specially before thee, O king Agrippa, that, after examination had, I might have somewhat to write.

27 For it seemeth to me unreasonable to send a prisoner, and not withal to signify [without stating] the crimes laid against him.

Paul's appeal to Rome had temporarily secured his safety. God said, "For I will shew him how great things he must suffer for my name's sake" (Acts 9:16).

28

Acts 26

The scene was set in the previous chapter. King Agrippa and Queen Bernice are seated awaiting Paul's hearing. The chief captains and principal men of the city were there also. Festus commands that Paul be brought before them. Here is another God-given opportunity to present his gospel. Upon receiving permission, Paul begins. Acts 26:1-3:

1 Then Agrippa said unto Paul, Thou art permitted to speak for thyself. Then Paul stretched forth the hand, and answered for himself:

2 I think myself happy, king Agrippa, because I shall answer for myself this day before thee touching all the things whereof I am accused of [by] the Jews:

3 Especially because I know thee to be expert in all customs and questions which are among the Jews: wherefore I beseech thee to hear me patiently.

Both King Agrippa and his queen were familiar with the customs and traditions of the Jews. Paul begins his defense by recounting his personal history. Verses 4-5:

4 My manner of life from my youth, which was at the first among mine own nation at Jerusalem, know all the Jews;

5 Which knew me from the beginning, if they would testify, that after the most straitest sect of our religion [for] I lived a Pharisee.

King Agrippa II was the grandson of Herod the Great who ordered that all male children two years of age and under be executed within the vicinity of Bethlehem. This was at the time of Jesus' birth. (See Matthew 2:16–18.) His father was Herod Agrippa I who accepted praise as being a god. Being filled with worms, his intestines burst. (See Acts 12:23.) King Agrippa II was familiar with the Jews and their intrigue. Therefore, Paul believed he would better understand his case. Verses 6-7:

6 And now I stand and am judged for the hope of the promise made of [by] God unto our fathers:

7 Unto which promise our twelve tribes, instantly serving God day and night, hope to come. For which hope's sake, king Agrippa, I am accused of [by] the Jews.

At this time, the Jews were still serving day and night at the Temple. Here was their "bone of contention." This "hope to come" was the crucial point of their disagreement. Verse 8:

8 Why should it be thought a thing incredible with you, that God should raise the dead?

Paul shares the details of his former life as a zealous follower of the Jewish religion. He was advancing above his peers and persecuting those who followed "the way." Verses 9-11:

9 I verily thought with myself, that I ought to do many things contrary to the name of Jesus of Nazareth. 10 Which thing I also did in Jerusalem: and many of the saints did I shut up in

prison, having received authority from the chief priests; and when they were put to death, I gave my voice against them.

11 And I punished them oft [often] in every synagogue, and compelled them to blaspheme; and being exceedingly mad against them, I persecuted them even unto strange [foreign] cities.

He recalls his sudden and unexpected encounter with the Risen Savior. At this point, his life changed forever. Verses 12-16:

12 Whereupon as I went to Damascus with authority and commission from the chief priests, 13 At midday, O king, I saw in the way [road] a light from heaven, above [greater than] the brightness of the sun, shining round about me and them which journeyed with me.

14 And when we were all fallen to the earth, I heard a voice speaking unto me, and saying in the Hebrew tongue, Saul, Saul, why persecutest thou me? it is hard for thee to kick against the

pricks. 15 And I said, Who art thou, Lord? And he said, I am Jesus whom thou persecutest.

16 But rise, and stand upon thy feet: for I have appeared unto thee for this purpose, to make thee a minister and a witness both of these things which thou hast seen, and of those things in the which I will appear unto thee;

God had spoken to Moses from a burning bush. It was from a brilliant light that exceeded the noonday sun that God spoke to Paul.

Do you remember Paul's speech before the crowd of Jews outside the castle? At the mere mention of the word "Gentiles," all hell broke loose. We are now at that point here. Paul is about to tell them the reason God chose him. Verses 17-18:

17 Delivering thee from the people, and from the Gentiles, unto whom now I send thee, 18 To open their eyes, and to turn them from darkness to light, and from the power of Satan unto God, that they may receive forgiveness of sins, and inheritance among them which are sanctified by faith that is in me.

There was no reaction from King Agrippa! Since he was familiar with much of what Paul was saying, there was no reaction. Paul continues. Verses 19-23:

19 Whereupon, O king Agrippa, I was not disobedient unto the heavenly vision: 20 But shewed first unto them of Damascus, and at Jerusalem, and throughout all the coasts of Judaea, and then to the Gentiles, that they should repent and turn to God, and do works meet [acceptable] for repentance.

21 For these causes the Jews caught me in the temple, and went about to kill me. 22 Having therefore obtained help of [from] God, I continue unto this day, witnessing both to small and great, saying none other things than those [things of] which the prophets and Moses did say should come:

23 That Christ should suffer, and that he should be the first that should rise from the dead, and should shew light unto the people [Israel], and to the Gentiles.

There is that word again, "Gentiles!" This time the reaction comes from Festus who, as a non-Jew, does not understand the Scriptures. Verse 24:

24 **And as he thus spake for himself, Festus said with a loud voice, Paul, thou art beside thyself; much learning doth make thee mad.**

Paul replies to Festus. Verses 25-26:

25 **But he said, I am not mad, most noble Festus; but speak forth the words of truth and soberness.**

26 **For the king knoweth of these things, before whom also I speak freely: for I am persuaded that none of these things are hidden from him; for this thing was not done in a corner.**

Paul knows that King Agrippa is knowledgeable of these things. Everything he said was not hidden in some obscure "corner." These facts were well known. He now speaks directly to the King. Verse 27:

27 **King Agrippa, believest thou the prophets? I know that thou believest.**

To this, the King responds. Verse 28:

> 28 **Then Agrippa said unto Paul, Almost thou persuadest me to be a Christian.**

Speaking on God's behalf, the Prophet Isaiah wrote the following. Isaiah 55:11:

> 11 **So shall my word be that goeth forth out of my mouth: it shall not return unto me void, but it shall accomplish that which I please, and it shall prosper in the thing whereto [the purpose for which] I sent it.**

There were many important people in that room, mostly Gentiles, who would have never heard Paul preach. God accomplished His purpose.

It would have greatly pleased Paul if they had responded by believing. Verse 29:

> 29 **And Paul said, I would [wish] to God, that not only thou, but also all that hear me this day, were both almost, and altogether such as I am, except these bonds.**

At this point, the meeting is adjourned when the King stood up. Verses 30-32:

> **30 And when he had thus spoken, the king rose up, and the governor, and Bernice, and they that sat with them: 31 And when they were gone aside, they talked between themselves, saying, This man doeth nothing worthy of death or of bonds.**

> **32 Then said Agrippa unto Festus, This man might have been set at liberty [free], if he had not appealed unto Caesar.**

We must remember that Paul's destiny was in the hands of God. "And we know that all things work together for good to them that love God, to them who are the called according to his purpose" (Romans 8:28). This we know for certain. Paul was called according to God's purpose.

29

Acts 27

After King Agrippa departed, Paul was placed in the custody of a centurion. He, along with other prisoners, was taken to a ship in Caesarea. It would carry them to Rome. The origin of the ship was from the port of Adramyttium, located on the coast of present-day Turkey. Acts 27:1-2:

1 And when it was determined that we should sail into Italy, they delivered Paul and certain other prisoners unto one named Julius, a centurion of Augustus' band.

2 And entering into a ship of Adramyttium, we launched, meaning [intending] to sail by the coasts of Asia; one Aristarchus, a Macedonian of Thessalonica, being with us.

Luke, the writer of Acts, was present on this trip as he used the pronoun "we" in verse 1. They set sail from the most eastern part of the Mediterranean Sea.

First, they sail north along the coast making a brief stop at Sidon for a change of cargo. While this took place, the centurion gave Paul permission to visit his friends there. When they continue on their voyage, they navigate west and sail under the Isle of Cyprus. This is where Paul stopped on his first missionary journey with Barnabas. Verses 3-4:

> 3 **And the next day we touched at Sidon. And Julius courteously entreated Paul, and gave him liberty to go unto his friends to refresh himself.**
>
> 4 **And when we had launched from thence, we sailed under Cyprus, because the winds were contrary [against us].**

They changed their course and sailed north until they came upon the coast of Asia Minor. Stopping at Myra, they were able to find a grain ship from Alexandria which was heading to Italy. They boarded this ship. Verses 5-6:

5 And when we had sailed over the sea of Cilicia and Pamphylia, we came to Myra, a city of Lycia.

6 And there the centurion found a ship of Alexandria sailing into Italy; and he put us therein.

There was a peninsula that jutted out from Asia Minor into the Aegean Sea which they had to sail around. However, the wind was against them. So, they sailed south passing along the shore of Crete. This island protected them from the winds. They reached the middle of the island where Fair Havens and Lasea were located. Verses 7-8:

7 And when we had sailed slowly many days, and scarce were come over against Cnidus, the wind not suffering [allowing] us, we sailed under Crete, over against Salmone;

8 And, hardly passing it, came unto a place which is called The fair havens; nigh [near] whereunto was the city of Lasea.

This was the season when traveling on the Mediterranean Sea could be dangerous. The prevailing winds now came from the northeast and there were violent storms. Paul makes a reference to "the fast was now already past." He refers to the Day of Atonement when all Jews must fast. Foul weather frequently occurs towards the end of September and beginning of October. Paul warns them to delay their voyage until the weather improves. Verses 9-10:

> 9 **Now when much time was spent, and when sailing was now dangerous, because the fast was now already past, Paul admonished them,**

> 10 **And said unto them, Sirs, I perceive that this voyage will be with hurt and much damage, not only of the lading and ship, but also of our lives.**

We cannot be sure if Paul's concern is from general knowledge or something from the Spirit. Either way, he must defer to the orders of the centurion. Because the harbor at Fair Haven was not suitable due to the size of the ship, they continued their course to Phoenix, called Phenice here. This port was located near the western end of the island which presently was their buffer from the storm. Verses 11-12:

11 Nevertheless the centurion believed the master [captain] and the owner of the ship, more than those things which were spoken by Paul.

12 And because the haven was not commodious [suitable] to winter in, the more part advised to depart thence also, if by any means they might attain to Phenice, and there to winter; which is an haven of Crete, and lieth toward the south west and north west.

They saw an opportunity when the winds died down to sailed close to the coast. They attempted to make their way to Phoenix located close to the end of the island. By doing so, they risked losing the wind protection of the island. The word "euroclydon" is a Greek word for "typhoon, tempest, or cyclone." They are known for their great winds and fierce waves. Verses 13-14:

13 And when the south wind blew softly, supposing that they had obtained their purpose, loosing thence, they sailed close by Crete. **14** But not long after there arose against it a tempestuous wind, called Euroclydon.

Alas, they lost the shelter of the island's protection and were now in the perils of the storm. No longer being able to control the ship, they let it take its own course. The winds blew them south of Crete away from the shore. Clauda or Klauda is an island due south of Phoenix. Verses 15-17:

> 15 **And when the ship was caught, and could not bear up into the wind, we let her drive.**
>
> 16 **And running under a certain island which is called Clauda, we had much work to come by [turn] the boat:**
>
> 17 **Which when they had taken up, they used helps, undergirding the ship; and, fearing lest they should fall into the quicksands, strake [immediately lowered the] sail, and so were driven.**

The sailors used "helps" which were ropes cast around the hull to "help" hold the framework together. Out of necessity, they allowed the ship to be driven by the wind and the waves. This was not unlike the storm Jonah faced in which the crew was terrified and, blaming him, cast Jonah overboard. (See Jonah 1:15-16.)

Imagine the fear of the fateful crew and the panic of the passengers. They threw the cargo overboard to lighten the ship. Still, the storm persisted against them. The third day, they began to jettison the ship's tackling. Verses 18-20:

18 And we being exceedingly tossed with a tempest, the next day they lightened the ship; 19 And the third day we cast out with our own hands the tackling of the ship.

20 And when neither sun nor stars in many days appeared, and no small tempest lay on us, all hope that we should be saved was then taken away.

Unable to see the sun or stars, they could not navigate the ship and lost their position. However, God knew exactly where they were and that Paul was a valuable passenger on this ship!

Let us stop and fix this situation in our minds. All of us have been in similar situations. Perhaps not as dire or life-threatening as this. When we find the reason for this misadventure, it show us something: All things do work together for good to them who love God and are called according to His purpose. (See Romans 8:28.) The next time any of us are in a dire situation, rather than panic, we should trust God.

The storm continued for so many days that those aboard the ship despaired. Verses 20-21:

> **20 And when neither sun nor stars in many days appeared, and no small tempest lay on us, all hope that we should be saved was then taken away.**
>
> **21 But after long abstinence Paul stood forth in the midst of them, and said, Sirs, ye should have hearkened unto me, and not have loosed from Crete, and to have gained this harm and loss.**

Paul was no ordinary man. He was an Apostle of God appointed by the Lord Jesus Christ Himself. He said this so they would remember they were in this mess because they did not listen to him. However, they should not despair. He had good news!

Remember, an angel is a messenger. Paul relates to the passengers the message he received. Verses 22-26:

> **22 And now I exhort you to be of good cheer: for there shall be no loss of any**

man's life among you, but of [only] the ship.

23 For there stood by me this night the angel of God, whose I am, and whom I serve, 24 Saying, Fear not, Paul; thou must be brought before Caesar: and, lo, God hath given thee all them that sail with thee.

25 Wherefore, sirs, be of good cheer: for I believe God, that it shall be even as it was told me. 26 Howbeit [Be it as it may] we must be cast upon a certain island.

Paul informs them that no one will be lost. However, to be saved, they must be driven or thrown upon an island. Although, at this point, they had no idea where they were.

It was now two weeks and they were still at sea being "driven up and down in Adria." The word "Adria" is short for the "Adriatic" Sea. This is part of the Mediterranean Sea with the Italian Peninsula on its left and the Balkan Peninsula on its right. Verses 27-29:

27 But when the fourteenth night was

come, as we were driven up and down in Adria, about midnight the shipmen deemed [believed] that they drew near to some country;

28 And sounded [measured the depth], and found it twenty fathoms [120 feet]: and when they had gone a little further, they sounded again, and found it fifteen fathoms [90 feet].

29 Then fearing lest we should have fallen upon rocks, they cast four anchors out of the stern, and wished for the day.

The purpose of these anchors was to slow the speed at which the boat was being driven by the wind and waves. This was important as they neared the shore.

The "not-so-fearless" crew were ready to abandon ship. The thought of being dashed upon the rocks had overwhelmed them. Paul spoke to the centurion and soldiers and explained to them what must be done. Verses 30-32:

30 And as the shipmen were about to flee out of the ship, when they had let

down the [life] boat into the sea, under colour [appearance] as though they would have cast anchors out of the foreship,

31 Paul said to the centurion and to the soldiers, Except these abide in the ship, ye cannot be saved. 32 Then the soldiers cut off the ropes of the [life] boat, and let her fall off.

As the crew were secretly trying to get off the ship, the soldiers came and cut the ropes. This let the lifeboat float away. This time they listened to Paul. Like the Ark that secured Noah and his family, they too were safe and secure within this Ark in God's care.

In preparation for their grounding, Paul tells everyone to eat something. They had not been eating for some time to conserve food. Now, they would need their strength. Verses 33-36:

33 And while the day was coming on, Paul besought them all to take meat [eat something], saying, This day is the fourteenth day that ye have tarried and continued fasting, having taken [eaten] nothing.

34 Wherefore I pray [ask] you to take some meat: for this is for your health: for there shall not an [one] hair fall from the head of any of you.

35 And when he had thus spoken, he took bread, and gave thanks to God in presence of them all: and when he had broken it, he began to eat. **36** Then were they all of good cheer, and they also took some meat [food].

Paul had changed their focus by thanking God. Those who were filled with fear now had faith in Paul's words. They believed him.

Until now, we had no idea how big this ship was. No wonder smaller harbors could not handle its size. There are 276 people aboard this ship. God assured Paul that not one person would be lost. Verses 37-38:

37 And we were in all in the ship two hundred threescore and sixteen souls. **38** And when they had eaten enough, they lightened the ship, and cast out the wheat into the sea.

This ship hailed from Egypt, a major exporter of

grain. Not only was the ship carrying passengers, but it was ladened with a store of grain. They desired to reduce the depth of its draft so the ship could be brought closer to the beach. So, they began disposing of its wheat. Verse 39:

> 39 **And when it was day, they knew not the land: but they discovered a certain creek with a shore, into the which they [decided] were minded, if it were possible, to thrust in the ship.**

The wind must have been blowing onshore. They had reduced the draft and determined their point of beaching. Now, they hoisted the mainsail to gain forward speed. Verse 40:

> 40 **And when they had taken up the anchors, they committed themselves unto the sea, and loosed the rudder bands, and hoised up the mainsail to the wind, and made toward shore.**

Heading directly toward the sandy beach, the boat struck it with some force so that it was securely lodged upon the shore. Verse 41:

> 41 **And falling into a place where two seas met, they ran the ship aground;**

and the forepart stuck fast, and remained unmoveable, but the hinder
part was broken with the violence of
the waves.

When a soldier takes custody of a prisoner, they
give their own life as a surety for their faithful de-
livery. For that reason, some of the soldiers wanted
to prevent the escape of the prisoners by killing
them. Verses 42-44:

42 And the soldiers' counsel was to kill
the prisoners, lest any of them should
swim out, and escape.

43 But the centurion, willing to save
Paul, kept them from their purpose;
and commanded that they which could
swim should cast themselves first into
the sea, and get to land:

44 And the rest, some on boards, and
some on broken pieces of the ship.
<u>And so it came to pass, that they es-
caped all safe to land.</u>

God remained true to His prediction to Paul. Not
one passengers was lost.

30

Acts 28

Imagine their joy! They fell face down on the beach, just glad to be alive. When they had no hope, it was Paul who restored it. He received a message from God and told the passengers the truth about the ship. Wait a minute! Is this not the same situation concerning Paul's gospel for salvation? God gave Paul the Gospel of Grace to be shared with Gentiles. It is God's plan for eternal life. Paul comes to people without hope and shares the message that brings the hope of salvation. For those who listen and believe, they will be saved.

The story continues concerning those who were saved. Acts 28:1-2:

> 1 **And when they were [had] escaped, then they knew [learned] that the island was called Melita.**

2 And the barbarous people shewed us no little kindness: for they kindled a fire, and received us every one, because of the present rain, and because of the cold.

These castaways were welcomed by the locals during the storm with much kindness. This island is now known by another name, Malta. If the map of Italy looks like a boot, then this island is close to the toe on the left side of Italy. They had arrived much closer to Rome than they thought.

In order to dry themselves and keep warm, Paul gathered wood for the fire. Verses 3-4:

3 And when Paul had gathered a bundle of sticks, and laid them on the fire, there came a viper out of the heat, and fastened on his hand.

4 And when the barbarians saw the venomous beast hang on his hand, they said among themselves, No doubt this man is a murderer, whom, though he hath escaped the sea, yet vengeance suffereth [allows] not to live.

The word "barbarian" was not as derogatory then

as it is today. Here, it means "a foreigner or some-one less civilized or unfamiliar with language, laws, or manners." Another injury to Paul occurs, this time with a venomous snake. How could God allow this to happen? There is a reason.

These were like the pagans Paul encountered in Ephesus. Notice how these non-believers react. They believe bad things happen to wicked people and viewed Paul's mishap as punishment for some-thing terrible he had done. Today, there are Chris-tians who think the same way. They believe that God is punishing the person when something bad happens to them. However, punishment comes from judgment. During this current Age of Grace, God is withholding judgment and punishment. He is offering His grace to everyone. All of Paul's epis-tles stress this fact. This is part of Paul's teaching. Everyone who wants to understand this current Age of Grace must understand what Paul is teach-ing!

Like many people today, we find people are ruled by superstition. Verses 5-6:

5 **And he shook off the beast into the fire, and felt no harm.**

6 **Howbeit they looked when he should**

have swollen, or fallen down dead suddenly: but after they had looked a great while, and saw no harm come to him, they changed their minds, and said that he was a god.

This is not unlike what happened to Paul and Barnabas in Lystra. When they healed a handicapped man, the heathen said, "The gods are come down to us in the likeness of men" (Acts 14:11). They called Barnabas the god Jupiter and Paul the god Mercury desiring to make sacrifices to them.

The leader on the island was named Publius. His father was ill and Paul healed him. News quickly spread throughout the small island so that others in need of healing came also. If Paul had not been diverted by the storm, then this never would have happened. Many situations similar to this may have caused Paul to write, "And we know that all things work together for good to them that love God, to them who are the called according to his purpose" (Rom. 8:28). Verses 7-9:

7 In the same quarters were possessions of the chief man of the island, whose name was Publius; who received us, and lodged us three days courteously.

8 And it came to pass, that the father of Publius lay sick of a fever and of a bloody flux: to whom Paul entered in, and prayed, and laid his hands on him, and healed him.

9 So when this was done, others also, which had diseases in the island, came, and were healed:

Out of gratitude, the people honored them and provided for their needs. Verse 10:

10 Who also honoured us with many honours; and when we departed, they laded [loaded] us with such things as were necessary.

They remained with these people for the three remaining months of winter. Then, in the spring, they took a ship to Syracuse, located on the nearby island of Sicily. Another ship arrived from Alexandria in Egypt. Castor and Pollux must refer to the ensign flown by this ship. These represented the twin half-brothers in Greek and Roman mythology. It would have been recognized in their region of commerce. Verses 11-12:

11 And after three months we departed

in a ship of Alexandria, which had wintered in the isle, whose sign was Castor and Pollux. 12 And landing at Syracuse, we tarried there three days.

From Syracuse, they traveled by ship to Rhegium which is located on the toe of the boot of Italy. Traveling north along the Italian coast, they arrived at their final port of Puteoli. It was located not far from Rome which was to the north and inland. Arriving there, Paul met brethren and stayed with them. I believe his Roman conductor had come to realize who Paul was and allowed him to visit there for a week. Verses 13-14:

13 And from thence we fetched a compass, and came to Rhegium: and after one day the south wind blew, and we came the next day to Puteoli: 14 Where we found brethren, and were desired to tarry with them seven days: and so we went toward Rome.

One of the Roman highways headed north to Rome. It was called the Via Appia. They traveled this route until they reached a marketplace called the Appii Forum. This was about forty-three miles southwest of Rome. Here, the brethren from Rome met them. Verse 15:

15 And from thence, when the brethren heard of us, they came to meet us as far as Appii forum, and The three taverns: whom when Paul saw, he thanked God, and took courage.

I believe Paul was aware of what laid ahead for him and he took courage when he saw the brethren.

Paul's journey to Rome would soon be completed. The Romans entrusted with the prisoners made the necessary transfers with one exception. Paul was not a prisoner. He was Roman citizen held for a trial and not convicted. He was allowed to dwell alone. Paul would eventually be moved to Caesar's palace, but for now, I believe the soldier who "kept him" was paid to house him. Verse 16:

16 And when we came to Rome, the centurion delivered the prisoners to the captain of the guard: but Paul was suffered [allowed] to dwell by himself with a soldier that kept him.

Only three days after his arrival in Rome, Paul contacted the local synagogue requesting a meeting. When they were together, Paul explained his situation. Verses 17-20:

17 **And it came to pass, that after three days Paul called the chief of the Jews together: and when they were come together, he said unto them, Men and brethren, though I have committed nothing against the people [Israel], or customs of our fathers, yet was I delivered [as a] prisoner from Jerusalem into the hands of the Romans.**

18 **Who, when they had examined me, would have let me go, because there was no cause of death in me.** 19 **But when the Jews spake against it, I was constrained to appeal unto Caesar; not that I had ought [anything] to accuse my nation of.**

20 **For this cause therefore have I called for you, to see you, and to speak with you: because that <u>for the hope of Israel I am bound with this chain</u>.**

When speaking of "the hope of Israel," he is referring to Jesus Christ, Israel's Messiah.

While in imprisoned Rome, he wrote this to Grace Believers in Philippi. His perseverance under duress caused other believers to become more bold in the sharing the gospel. Philippians 1:13-14:

> 13 So that <u>my bonds in Christ</u> are manifest [made known] in all the palace, and in all other places; 14 And many of the brethren in the Lord, waxing [growing] confident by my bonds, are much <u>more bold to speak the word</u> without fear.

Paul was the pattern or model that God intended other Grace Believers to follow. (See 1 Tim. 1:16.)

The Jews from the synagogue in Rome respond in Acts 28:21-22:

> 21 And they said unto him, We neither received letters out of Judaea concerning thee, neither any of the brethren that came shewed or spake any harm of thee.

> 22 But we desire to hear of [from] thee what thou thinkest: for as concerning this sect, we know that everywhere it is spoken against.

Even though it was spoken against all over, they wanted to hear more. So, Paul arranged a time when they could meet again. Verse 23:

> 23 And when they had appointed him a day, there came many to him into his lodging; to whom he expounded and testified the kingdom of God, persuading them concerning Jesus, both out of the law of Moses, and out of the prophets, from morning till evening.

Although these Jews were educated in the Scripture, they always look for something to debate. Each individual would present his own thoughts and ideas. It may have been more about showing their own knowledge of Scripture than understanding what Paul presented.

It appears that Paul wasted his time. He quotes a prophecy which was given to Israel by the Prophet Isaiah over 700 years ago. Verses 24-27:

> 24 And some believed the things which were spoken, and some believed not.
>
> 25 And when they agreed not among themselves, they departed, after that Paul had spoken one word, Well spake the Holy Ghost by Esaias [Isaiah] the prophet unto our fathers,

26 Saying, Go unto this people, and say, Hearing ye shall hear, and shall not understand; and seeing ye shall see, and not perceive:

27 For the heart of this people is waxed gross, and <u>their ears are dull of hearing</u>, and <u>their eyes have they closed</u>; lest they should see with their eyes, and hear with their ears, and understand with their heart, and should be converted, and I should heal them.

If there is anyone who does not believe there are two separate gospels, as revealed in Scripture, then they need to carefully consider the following proclamation. Verse 28:

28 Be it known therefore unto you, that <u>the salvation of God is sent unto the Gentiles, and that they will hear it</u>.

Christ brought the good news of the Gospel of the Kingdom. His Twelve Apostles were entrusted with that gospel message. This is the same gospel that will be preached again after the Rapture. But now, in this present Age of Grace, the gospel message is different. It is sent to the Gentiles and any who will listen. It is the Gospel of Grace of which Paul was made the Apostle.

As the Jews continued to argue and reason among themselves, the Gentiles rejoiced that salvation had now come to them. Verses 29-31:

> 29 And when he had said these words, the Jews departed, and had great reasoning among themselves.

> 30 And Paul dwelt two whole years in his own hired house, and received all that came in unto him,

> 31 Preaching the kingdom of God, and teaching those things which concern the Lord Jesus Christ, with all confidence, no man forbidding him.

Epilogue

The Acts of the Apostles is an historical summary. It records the works or actions of the apostles following the death, burial, and resurrection of the Lord Jesus Christ. The New Testament is not like a novel where one chapter follows the other chronologically. Because Acts is a summary, other books of the New Testament were written during the timeline recorded by Acts. These other books, called epistles, are letters written by apostles to particular assemblies or groups of believers. Since there are two gospel messages, these epistles are divided into two groups: the Pauline Epistles and the Hebrew Epistles.

The first group of letters, the Pauline Epistles, follow the book of Acts. There are thirteen letters written by the Apostle Paul to Grace Believers. As discussed earlier, their salvation is a gift given by God and received through faith in the Word of God. Following the Gospel of Grace, they believe and trust solely in the finished work of Jesus' death, burial, and resurrection. This gospel was sent to the Gentiles, but anyone who believes, whether Jew or Gentile, can receive salvation as a gift. The Pauline Letters begin with Romans and end with Philemon.

The second group of letters, known as the Hebrew Epistles, are written to Kingdom Believers. There are eight not including Revelation. They are written to the remnant of Israel who believe the Kingdom Gospel. They affirm that Jesus Christ is their Messiah and the Son of God. Following the Gospel of the Kingdom preached by Jesus Christ and the Twelve, they must keep the Mosaic Law and all the commandments. They must repent of their sins, be baptized, continue to do good works as proof of their faith, and endure unto the end. Doing so, their sins are in remission and they will receive their salvation at the return of their Messiah. Kingdom Believers must endure the Tribulation as a test of their faith. Whereas, Grace Believers will be removed at the Rapture prior to the Tribulation.

Currently, as of this writing, we are in the Age of Grace. God is withholding His judgment and offering amnesty to all who will accept His terms. At the end of the Age of Grace, God will withdrawal His gracious offer of salvation. Its withdrawal is imminent and could occur at any time. When will the Age of Grace end? The only clue comes from Paul. We learned that God turned from the Jews temporarily to the Gentiles. (See Acts 28:28.). He writes to the Grace Believers in Rome explaining the answer to this very question. Romans 11:25:

> 25 **For I would not, brethren, that ye should be ignorant of this mystery, lest ye should be wise in your own conceits; that blindness in part is happened to Israel, <u>until the fulness of the Gentiles be come in.</u>**

The present Age of Grace began with the salvation of Paul who said he was "chief among sinners" meaning he was the worst of the worst. If God could save Paul, the worst of the worst. then He can save anyone! Paul is the "pattern" all others who are saved by grace should follow. We should follow him, because he followed Christ. (See 1 Timothy 1:14-16.)

I must be careful as a teacher of the Bible, my favorite subject. I get excited, but must not try to put eight hours of teaching into a sixty-minute class. So, I will end with some recommendations. There is an introductory book titled *The Hidden Gospel*. It is a small book and designed as an introduction to the dividing the Bible into seven dispensations. Dispensations are only tools to help you understand the Bible – like fences divide one large pasture.

For more committed students of the Bible, I recommend two summary books to my students. I call them "two sides of the same coin" where the Bible is represented by the coin. The first book, titled *Letters to Theophilus,* looks at the entire Bible dispensationally focusing on the Gentiles. The second book also looks at the entire Bible dispensationally, but it focuses on Israel's promises and prophecies. The title of this book is *The Glorious Destiny of Israel.* As a Dean of Graduate Students, I believe these two books together would be equal to a seminary's graduate level course in Systematic Theology. They provide a solid foundation for understanding the Bible dispensationally.

Finally, commentaries can be excellent. They can provide a guide for the individual books of the Bible. I did not always agree with the commentaries I was required to read. However, I had to defend my position as to why I disagreed. GraceWord has a number of commentaries on the New Testament. They are part of growing series called A Grace Expositional Commentary. Each walks you through a book of the Bible verse-by-verse providing an interpretation supported by other biblical references.

These systematic summaries and individual commentaries provide a methodical approach leading to a solid grasp of God's Word. Remember, you are free to either agree or disagree, but be able to support your interpretation with biblical verses. Over the years, I have heard people support their beliefs by saying, "Well, Calvin says," or "But, Augustine says," or "my pastor says." Do not fall prey to human traditions, customs, or philosophies. Allow the Bible to speak for itself.

I will end with a warning that Paul wrote to the Grace Believers in Colossae. It had to do with Who they should trust for understanding doctrine. Colossians 2:8-10:

> **8 Beware lest any man spoil you through philosophy and vain deceit, after the tradition of men, after the rudiments of the world, and not after Christ.**
>
> **9 For in him dwelleth all the fulness of the Godhead bodily.**
>
> **10 And ye are complete in him, which is the head of all principality and power:**

Resources

Here are some resources I would recommend. My dear friends Steve and Stephanie Tackett offer many resources. Steve has taught rightly dividing the Word of Truth for many years. He breaks the Bible down and explains it dispensationally. He has written two of the books in the Grace Expositional Commentary Series. They offer live weekly online Bible classes, recorded classes, and audio recordings through Grace Bible Network. Their website is: www.gracebiblenetwork.org.

The Berean Bible Society has been helping people to understand right division since 1940. They mail out a free monthly publication called *The Berean Searchlight*. All you have to do is sign up for it online. They offer free online classes, have a bookstore, and host regional Bible conferences as well. Their website is: www.bereanbiblesociety.org.

There is a list of Grace Assemblies preaching the Word of God rightly divided. As of this writing, the list is maintained and updated regularly. Their website is: www.gracechurches.wordpress.com.

Finally, you can check out the list of other publications from GraceWord Publishing. Their website is: www.gracewordpublishing.com. There is a Contact Us option on the website.

Other GraceWord Publications

About The Author

Dr. David Alan Greene has over thirty-five years of experience as an insurance agent selling both property and casualty as well as life insurance. During his career, he taught and explained the content and meaning of policies to his clients. Now retired, he devotes much of his time to teaching the Bible.

He obtained his Bachelor of Theology, Master of Biblical Studies, and Ph.D. in Biblical Studies from Evangelical Theological Seminary where he holds the position of Dean of Graduate Studies. He also holds a Ph.D. in Christian Counseling. He has written numerous biblical commentaries and books on rightly dividing the Word of Truth.